Maine

This collection of essays brings together the writings of Fannie Hardy Eckstorm, Manly Hardy, Thomas Wentworth Higginson, and the poetry of Anna Boynton Averill. Through their words, they share their connections to, and a love for, the Maine north woods.

Those who explore the waters and woods across Maine know well the beauty and history the state holds, and these stories, poems, and legends add to the fascinating facts about this captivating land.

A
Burnt Jacket Publishing
Classic Release

Katahdin, Pamola

&

Whiskey Jack

Stories & Legends

from

The Maine Woods

Edition Compiled

by

Tommy Carbone

ANNOTATED EDITION

Cover photo, and newly added interior illustrations, and photos from the collection of Tommy Carbone, or as otherwise noted.

Author of new material and edition editor, Tommy Carbone.

**Katahdin, Pamola & Whiskey Jack –
Stories & Legends from The Maine Woods**

Burnt Jacket Publishing
Greenville, Maine
Copyright 2021

20231020ISPB

ISBN: 978-1-954048-20-1

www.tommycarbone.com

1. *Maine woods - 2. Canoeing - 3. Camping - 4. Expeditions and adventure*
5. *Memoir - 6. Naturalist - 7. Hunting and fishing. - 8. Woodsmen –*
9. *19th Century History - 10. Katahdin.*

Contents

Edition Photographs

About the advertisements:

In the days books such as this were originally published, they included many advertisements as sponsorship to the cost of printing. In this book, advertisements have been selected from the time period that would have been found in magazines such as *Forest and Stream*. While the establishments no longer exist, they provide a stamp on the period of Maine history and add to the nostalgia of the writing.

Introduction

It was not too long ago when the mountains, lakes, and rivers of Maine were the domain of a few. They were the map makers, the timber cruisers, the trappers, and the woodsmen. The map makers may have been sent on a mission from the King of England to identify boundaries. The timber cruisers were employed by land owners wishing to find the remaining pockets of great pines. The trappers and the woodsmen ventured deep into the forest to hunt; these were men who, like Manly Hardy, were well known in the 1800s for their woodcraft knowledge and expertise. Manly Hardy's connection to the outdoors was first, for his livelihood, but also as a documenter of the ways of the Maine woods. He kept meticulous journals on his exploring and wrote numerous contributions to the sportsmen magazines of his day. He was a well-respected 'voice of the woods,' and in 1901 the editor of *Forest and Stream* wrote, "No one is more familiar with the wild animals of Maine than Mr. Manly Hardy, the veteran woodsman and traveler of Brewer, Maine."

The outdoor experiences with her father provided the starting point for the writing of Fannie Hardy Eckstorm. The woods became her laboratory where she observed animals and catalogued stories and legends that were told to her. She would go on to become a respected nature writer, and her contributions to magazines. such as *Forest and Stream*, were widely read.

This volume of essays is connected by two threads. The first being 'the outdoors of Maine,' and second, the Hardy family contributions to the state's long history of outdoor explorers and naturalists. It is a volume of interesting articles and letters to further celebrate the writings of Fannie Hardy Eckstorm and her father, Manly Hardy, that was started in, *Exploring the Maine Woods – The Hardy Family Expedition to the Machias Lakes.*

In that prior book, I included selections from the poems of Anna Boynton Averill. Readers remarked that they would enjoy reading more of Averill's poems. I myself have found in reading the prose of Averill, I am transported to my favorite places in the woods. For these reasons, entire Averill poems are included in this book.

The selection of Eckstorm essays that form the main basis for this book were published in *Forest and Stream* in 1889 and 1890 under the title, *Out of Door Papers.* To these essays I have added references and notes to provide additional background for the reader. In addition to these writings, the book includes other essays from Eckstorm, her father, Manly Hardy, as well as a story written by Thomas Wentworth Higginson on his climb of Mount Katahdin.

I am once again grateful to the Special Collections Department at the Raymond H. Fogler Library of the University of Maine in Orono. The university holds the, *"Fannie Hardy Eckstorm Paper Collection, 1865-1946,"* which proved to be a valuable resource in compiling this book.

Overall, Manly Hardy and Fannie Hardy Eckstorm left a legacy of which Mainers can be proud. I am pleased to bring these writings once again into publication. Enjoy the stories from the Maine north woods.

Tommy Carbone
Greenville, Maine   July 2021

Fannie Pearson Hardy Eckstorm
(1865 – 1946)

Eckstorm in 1888, the year of her college graduation.

Image courtesy of Special Collections, Raymond H. Fogler Library, University of Maine

Fannie Pearson Hardy Eckstorm was born on June 18, 1865, in Brewer, Maine to Manly Hardy and Emmeline Wheeler Hardy. She was the oldest of their six children and attended the public schools in Brewer, Maine and Abbot Academy (Andover, MA). In 1888, she graduated from Smith College (North Hampton, MA), was subsequently employed as the superintendent of schools in Brewer, and for a time worked in the book department of the D.C. Heath Publishing Company in Boston.

In 1893 she married Rev. Jacob A. Eckstorm of Chicago. Seven years later, following the passing of her husband,

Fannie Eckstorm and her two children relocated from Providence R.I., back to Brewer, Maine.

Throughout her life, Eckstorm studied Maine Indians, folklore and natural history. It was an area she knew well, based on her experiences with her father in the woods and her personal acquaintance with the Native Americans and woodsmen. This book is only one example of her deep knowledge in these subjects.

In 1886 she became an associate member of the American Ornithologists Union, the first woman admitted as such. Before graduating Smith College, she co-founded the college chapter of the Audubon Society. Her interest in birds would be a lifelong pursuit, from which she published two books, *The Woodpeckers* (1901) and *The Bird Book* (1901).

She had a deep interest in documenting Maine folksongs and woods songs, and in collaboration with others, two books resulted from her efforts, *Minstrelsy of Maine* (1927) and *British Ballads from Maine* (1929).

Eckstorm had many other community interests, among them, she was a founder and vice-president of the Folk-Song Society of the Northeast, a founding member of the public library in Brewer, and was an honorary member of the Maine Historical Society.

Other books written by Fannie Hardy Eckstorm are:
- The Penobscot Man (1904).
  - Annotated Edition, "The Penobscot Man – Life and Death on a Maine River," Tommy Carbone, Burnt Jacket Publishing, 2022.
- David Libbey: Penobscot Woodsman and River-Driver, (1907).

- Annotated Edition, "David Stone Libbey – He Was Penobscot," Tommy Carbone, Burnt Jacket Publishing, 2022.
- Of Indian Place-Names of the Penobscot Valley and the Maine Coast (1941).
- Old John Neptune and Other Maine Indian Shamans (1945).
- Fannie Hardy Eckstorm – Short Stories and Essays – Compiled and Annotated by Tommy Carbone (2023).

Eckstorm also wrote for magazines such as *Forest and Stream*, *Sprague's Journal of Maine History*, *The Northern*, *The New England Quarterly*, *The Atlantic Monthly* and other publications and newspapers. Her knowledge was well respected by readers and she was never one to shy away from controversy in dealing with facts in her writing, or correcting others. The style of her writing is genuine and her documenting of Maine history has been trusted for over a century.

On December 31, 1946 Fannie Hardy Eckstorm passed away. She had been residing in the same home in Brewer since moving there in 1900. She was 81 years young.

A Maine Pond
(Editor's Collection)

Manly Hardy

(1832 – 1910)

Manly Hardy was born on November 11, 1832, in Hampden, Maine, the only child of Jonathan Titcomb Hardy and Catherine Sears Atwood Hardy. The family moved to Brewer, Maine, when Manly was four, and he remained there for the rest of his life.

He attended the public schools, and for advanced studies attended the private school conducted by the Rev. George W. Field, D. D., in Bangor. Early in life Mr. Hardy injured his eyes (said to be from study at night), and for many years could not read at all. He was said to have a remarkable memory.

He became a fur buyer and dealer, maintaining one of the most extensive fur businesses in Maine. He spent much of his time in the woods of Maine, acquiring an expansive knowledge of woodlore and developing friendships with other men familiar with the wilderness, including the local Indians, to whom he could converse in their language. Overall, he was an expert woodsman.

He was a hunter of deer, moose and bear, and was also fond of hunting seals and porpoises from a canoe, a sport which was often dangerous, and likely always to be full of excitement. He made a long study of the ruffed grouse, and was one of the first authorities in the United States on this bird.

In 1861 he was the assistant naturalist on the Maine State Scientific Survey. He began to mount birds and assembled a collection of some 3,300 U.S. birds. He became the most widely known naturalist of Maine in his time, and was an honorary member of the Maine Ornithological Society. He also wrote extensively about the Maine woods, Indians, and mammals.

The following was written about him in a 1910 issue of *Forest and Stream*. "Mr. Hardy's stern love of truth has sometimes led him to correct sharply in print statements which he knew were incorrect, and it has been in such critical writings that his name has most often been seen. Yet it is not his nature to find fault. On the contrary, he is a genial, humorous and wholly friendly man, who would much rather praise than blame, yet, as we conceive, possesses the simple feeling that, no one is entitled to especial credit for telling the simple truth."

This quote is important because his daughter also called upon facts to correct what she saw as errors that writers had made. A few examples are given in this book.

While Manly Hardy kept meticulous journals and wrote several magazine pieces, Fannie Hardy wrote this about her father:

"Of his writing I may mention one characteristic. He never overstated. His two longest writings, each of which filled several installments of Forest and Stream, 'A Maine Woods Walk in '61' and 'A Fall Fur Hunt,' might have been much

expanded if he had chosen to dilate upon his incidents. But he condensed as much as possible even while telling a story. I remonstrated with him upon this. 'I didn't want to make the broth too thick,' was his characteristic response."

He married Emmeline Freeman Wheeler on December 24, 1862. They had six children: Fannie Hardy Eckstorm, Catherine Atwood Hardy Bates, Annie Eliza Hardy Eckstorm, Manly Willis Hardy, who lived less than two years, and twins Charlotte W. Hardy and Walter M. Hardy.

Manly Hardy died on December 9, 1910.

- - - - - - -

The information for the profile of Manly Hardy comes from several sources, with the majority from a profile written by Mrs. Eckstorm in tribute to her father:

Eckstorm, Fannie Hardy, "Manly Hardy," The Journal of the Maine Ornithological Society, Vol. XIII, No. I., March 1911, Pg. 1-9.

Walter Hardy

Walter M. Hardy (1877 – 1933) was an artist, writer, and owner of a Maine apple orchard. The son of Manly Hardy, he was born in Brewer on February 9, 1877, and after graduating from Bangor High School in 1896, he spent a year at the University of Maine before transferring to the Art Students League in New York City. He also studied in Paris, England, and Italy. Like his father, he was interested in birds and other wildlife. After his return to the U.S., he did illustrations of birds and animals for various publications. He also illustrated some of the articles written by his father. In 1911, he bought a farm in Holden, Maine, where he planted a large apple orchard. He raised and sold apples there until his death on September 17, 1933.

Anna Boynton Averill

Poems by Anna Boynton Averill (1843 – 1915) are included as Averill's poems about the Maine north woods are appropriate for this book, the time period, and the verses compliment the essays.

Averill, was an accomplished poet who had a large collection of her poems published in a book, "Birch Stream And Other Poems," (1908). She was born in Alton, Maine and as of the 1870 census was employed as a teacher and living in the town of Dover in Piscataquis County.

Maine Map

Map of Maine.

A Carrying Place
(Editor's Collection)

I — The Collection

WITHIN these pages are essays written about the Maine woods from the mid-1800s to the early 1900s. The collection has been selected by the editor for the theme of the Maine forest, legends, and history.

The book centers around the writing of Fannie Hardy Eckstorm, who established herself as a writing talent following her college years. During that time, she contributed articles to magazines, such as *Forest and Stream* and *The Atlantic*. A series of her essays appeared under the title, *Out-of-Door Papers*, in the *Forest and Stream* issues of 1889 and 1890. This series pre-dated her 1891 contribution titled, *In the Region Round Nicatowis*, which has been published in the annotated edition, *Exploring the Maine Woods – The Hardy Family Expedition to the Machias Lakes (Burnt Jacket Publishing, 2021)*.

These selections from her *Out-of-Door Papers*, illustrate her love of the outdoors, wildlife, history, and literature. Her appreciation for wildlife was from both the naturalist observer and in the case of birds, also as an ornithologist and taxidermist – roles she was able to distinctly separate given time, location, and purpose.

Essay selections for this book, include the description of being windbound on a shore of Chamberlain Lake, the observed preference of the sapsucker for certain trees, the solitude of winter ice fishing on a Maine lake, her observations of the birds near a tiny brook (or brooklet as Eckstorm so calls it), and her opining on dried poplar as a campfire wood; a piece that is brilliant for those who have camped in the wilds of Maine.

A large part of Eckstorm's writing, here and elsewhere, is about birds. Considering her father, with her assistance, collected over 3000 specimens, she had many opportunities to question and learn about the habits of the winged species. In an essay labeled, *Largely Personal*, she covers her experiences with owls. At the conclusion of her essay, Manly Hardy offers his expertise on owls.

If there is a singular essay that provided the inspiration for this book, it would be *Concerning the Bad Repute of Whiskey John*. Eckstorm's writing on a bird with many names is not only entertaining, but informative. The thievery of Jack is as true today, as when the piece was first penned.

In each essay the writer's skill in observation and making connections is woven into interesting stories that are about Maine, with topics that can generally be applied to the *out of doors* anywhere, for which the reader will easily connect.

Eckstorm had many passions for Maine – the wildlife, the history of lumbermen and woodsmen, and the preservation of ballads, which told stories through words that often read like poetry. However, she had a special passion for preserving the original names of locations in Maine, and also what she considered important generational stories and legends. Eckstorm, and her father, had many acquaintances who were Native American. These friends, whom they traveled the woods with and visited their homes, relayed legends and experiences from the Maine woods. It is not surprising then that Eckstorm would document the most complete essay on the legends of the state's largest mountain.   Long before the Appalachian Trail was an idea, or the boundaries of Baxter State Park were drawn, Mount Katahdin was loved, revered, and, by some, feared. Eckstorm, through her association with Native Americans catalogued stories about the mountain and the associated spirit that was said to live within. In her method of exactness, she has compiled, as well as critiqued, what others have told her, or written, in her essay, *Legends of Katahdin*.

Over the years, Eckstorm mentioned Katahdin in various articles and letters, in particular during her time spent exploring the regions of the Penobscot River, and again in her essay on Thoreau. A 1908 letter from Thomas Wentworth Higginson to Eckstorm provides an interesting introduction to an essay Higginson wrote for *Putnam's Magazine* in 1856 on his climb of Maine's tallest mountain. His complete essay is included in this volume for his wit and the historical significance of that trip.

Katahdin is not solely the subject of stories and legends. In her poem, *Birch Stream*, Anna Boynton Averill gives tribute to Katahdin: "*Northward Katahdin's chasmed pile Looms through thy low, long, leafy aisle.*" Averill, a northern Maine native wrote verses about known places across the north woods. Her poems are the perfect complement to the theme of this book.

A book about the woods of Maine would not be complete without descriptions of wildlife. Two selections from the writings of Manly Hardy provide us with his keen insight to Otters and Panthers. Additionally, his, *On Not Getting Lost in the Woods* essay stirred a good deal of controversy at the time, and his warnings are as applicable now, as they were then.

The writings from Fannie Hardy Eckstorm and Manly Hardy would not be complete without controversy. Eckstorm, in her usual way, provides us an education on the Indian names of Kokadjo and Bagaduce; while Manly Hardy contributed to the controversy in a year-long debate in *Forest and Stream* over a Rudyard Kipling poem. These writings provide a glimpse into the Hardy family expectations that the history and meaning of woodlore and place names be correctly documented and retained for future generations to know the origins.

Several illustrations from Walter Manly Hardy are included in this book. These have been restored from the McClure's Magazine article, *A Tale of the Trout Stream (1901)*, by William Davenport Hulbert. While Walter Hardy was an active artist early in his life, many of his works are unknown and can no longer be located.

You may already explore off the beaten path in the north woods of Maine, if so, this collection of essays and poems may stir some memories of the solitude you experience while there. Or, maybe you watch and enjoy the songs of the birds right from your window. However you appreciate the outdoors, such reflection and appreciation of this beauty can have beneficial effects. As Eckstorm has written: *"These are the events of the day, so few and unimportant that it seems time lost to chronicle them, and yet of what are most of our days made up of?"*

Go *Out-of-Doors* and observe the wonder of
The Maine Woods.

II — Over The Hills And Far Away

by
Anna Boynton Averill

We know by the leaves and the bending grasses
That the wind of the south goes by today,
A viewless spirit that softly passes
"Over the hills and far away."

On its wings of balm we fain would follow
Through greenwood deeps at our will to stray,
Or aloft on the track of the tireless swallow,
"Over the hills and far away."

For from toiling town and from sleepy hollow,
We lift our eyes to the hills and pray,
O, with the wind and the bird to follow
"Over the hills and far away!"

Over the Hills and Far Away
(Editor's Collection)

III — The Katahdin Legends

THIS essay, like many from Eckstorm, is written in her definitive style and captures the legends of Katahdin as they were told to her. Her intent was to chronicle the history of the Maine woods based on fact and direct evidence from her research and interviews. The essay is one of the most complete summaries of the Katahdin and Pamola legends that has ever been written. Whether you've been to Katahdin or not, after reading you may never consider Maine's most majestic mountain in the same way again.

The Katahdin Legends
A public domain work, once published in,
Appalachia, Appalachian Mountain Club *(Boston),*
Vol. 18, No 4, December 1924.

"Ev'ry mountain he got Injun in it. Katahdin, he man. Bahmolai (Pamola) he diff'rent —no body, only leetle mite here"— and my Old Lady drew a small circle with her forefinger upon her ample bosom — "all legs, hands. Katahdin, he diff'rent, mountain once was man."

This, in the very words of the oldest member of the Penobscot tribe, taken down while she was speaking,[1] eight years ago, is the Indian's own idea of what is generally considered the presiding genius of Katahdin.

What an Indian thinks, and what a white man thinks the Indian is thinking, are often two very unlike concepts. Nor does it help much when the Indian, for lack of English words, gives the same name to several very different ideas. Again, whenever the Indian does not wish to reveal his inmost thoughts, he puts the white man off with a "pacifier." The more one knows Indians, the less he accepts from them without checking it up. The word *Pamola*, as the whites have usually written the Indian *Bumole* (which they pronounce *Bahmolai*), stands for three entirely unlike Indian conceptions. One of them is *Bumole*, the spirit of the night wind, which my Old Lady was describing; one is the Storm-bird; and one is the giant Katahdin, of human figure, who dwells inside the mountain. One is almost harmless, one is hideously destructive, one is rather friendly; but to the white man they are all Pamola.

Without pretending to be a student of folklore, and so passing no judgments in a field not my own, I wish to collate the versions of the Katahdin myths drawn from aboriginal sources, to make as clear as I can the Indian conceptions, and to add a little that I have gleaned in a long acquaintance with the Penobscot Indians.

---

[1] Eckstorm is referring to Clara Neptune, who Eckstorm interviewed with the purpose of documenting Penobscot history.

The most widely known version of the Katahdin legends is that of Father Vetromile,[2] an Italian priest, for some years resident in Oldtown. What Father Vetromile knew about Indians has been much overrated. His linguistic acquirements were not large, and his high-handed interference in an Indian political quarrel, started long before his coming, gave him the ill-will of about half of the Penobscot tribe, so that much of the information they gave him is unreliable. For example, in connection with his Katahdin legend, the name "Lake Amboctictus," for Ambajejus Lake, with the indecent meaning assigned in a footnote, was only one of their wholly successful attempts to fool the holy father. The qualifications of the reverend father as a folklorist are exemplified in this remark (not quoted by Sprague): "The appearance of God to Moses in the Burning Bush may be glimpsed in Pamole appearing to the Indian on Mount Katahdin, and so forth."

Charles G. Leland[3] notes that Vetromile's version of the legend is corrupted, and that two very different beings, Bumole and the Spirit of Mount Katahdin, are confounded. Yet though having a very poor opinion of Father Vetromile's knowledge of the Indians and their language, I do not hold him responsible for confusing these two beings. For a very long time the Indians themselves had been giving the name of

---

[2] *The Abnakis and their History*, by Rev. Eugene Vetromile, S. J., New York, 1866. Quoted in Sprague's *Journal of Maine History*, Vol. 10, No. 4 (1922), pp. 215-220; and again, slightly altered, without Vetromile's name, in *Sebastian Rale*, by Hon. John Francis Sprague (New York, 1906), pp. 93 - 98. Also, De Costa's Mount Desert, second ed., 1871, and many other references.

[3] Algonquin Legends of New England (Boston, 1884), p. 257.

Pamola to all versions of the mountain legends; and years before Vetromile came, Pamola was the conventional name among the whites for all the Katahdin spirits. We need only quote from Rev. Marcus Keep's account of his visit to the Basin of Katahdin, September 18, 1847:[4]

So far as I can learn, I was the first human visitor to this fabled residence of the Indians' Pamolah. It is not strange that a superstitious people should have many traditions of his wonderful pranks, and be kept away from close engagement with such a foe. When we reach the lake on our way to Ktaadn, it is easy to see the origin of those fears which the Indians are said to have respecting the mountain as the residence of Pamolah, or Big Devil. Clouds form in the basin, and are seen whirling out in all directions. Tradition tells a "long yarn" about a "handsome squaw" among the Penobscots, who once did a great business in slaying her thousands among the young chiefs of her nation, but was finally taken by Pamolah to Ktaadn, where he now protects himself and his prize from approaching Indians with all his artillery of thunder and hail.

The Indian says that it is "sartin true, 'cause handsome squaw always ketch um debble"; whether this be true or not, the basin is the birthplace of storms, and

---

[4] In the *Bangor Democrat*, Dec. 9, 1847; reprinted with interpolations by another person, perhaps Rev. J. R. Munsell, one of the party, in *Forest Life and Forest Trees*, by John S. Springer (Harper and Bros., New York, 1851), p. 193.

I have myself heard the roar of its winds for several miles.

This, evidently taken directly from an Indian, is a very loose rendering. Pamola never was regarded as "Big Devil," or *Matchehant*; but where can one equal the cynicism of this unknown Indian, whose proof that his story is true is that "the Devil always gets the handsome women"?

Probably contemporary, though not put in print until 1919, is what an old man of Staceyville, Mr. Dudley, said he heard Governor John Neptune tell when he was a child.[5]

This old man's saying that he could remember back "well over seventy years," taken with Governor Neptune's death in 1865 at the age of ninety-seven, makes the date of the story not far from 1845. Mr. Curl writes:

It is not to be wondered that the Indians peopled the mountains with Pamola, the fierce, avenging spirit who relished their destruction. Old John Neptune, famous Oldtown Indian of other days, called upon the Dudley family years ago, when Mr. Dudley was a mere little lad, and related his experiences with the fury of the mountain. "Folks say no Pamola, if they want to," he said, "but I know; I see him. Ol' Pamola there all right."

---

[5] Melvin J. Curl, "Climbing Ktaadn." *Boston Sunday Herald*, Nov. 16, 1919. (About Mark Dudley. See also inset on his son, Leroy Dudley.)

He told how, though he had been warned against the deed, he went up into the mountain to hunt and stayed overnight in a shack with a strong door. In the night, when John was asleep, Pamola swooped down from his fastnesses in the crags and alighted in the yard by the shack, a great beast, with mighty wings that dragged on the ground, with a head as large as four horses, and with horrible beak and claws. He beat upon the door of the shack, and roared and howled and heaved again and again at the fastenings, but by good luck the door was frozen down and he could not budge it. So, with a last, long yell of rage and defiance, he flapped filthily and wickedly away. Four other Indians whom John knew, less fortunate, went into the mountain and never returned. Pamola got them somewhere. John had seen the entrance to Pamola's cave, and knew where, in the northwest basin, he hung out his lantern of nights, before his den, where he crawled with his prey.

Some of the details of this story, like that of the lantern, would not have occurred to an Indian; still, in the main, it is genuine and ancient. It may seem strange, when for more than fifty years John Neptune was the friend of my grandfather and father, and for about twenty years he lived so near that he was almost a daily visitor, that no hint of this story has come down in our family. It may seem stranger that when the old Indian woman, who for ten years imparted to me what she knew of Indian tradition, was the widow of John Neptune's grandson, she never told me anything about this experience of the old Governor. It is strangest that George H. Hunt, the man who has known more Penobscot Indians well than any man who ever lived, having been Indian agent and trader for most of his long life, should tell me two days ago that he knew nothing about this Storm-bird and had no Indian name for it. But this negative evidence proves only that an Indian will not always tell his best friend what he believes in. A hundred years ago Judge Williamson, who knew Indians well, showed that he had heard much the same that John Neptune said, quite likely from Neptune himself. He wrote: "They say that Pamola is very great and very strong, indeed; that his head and face is like a man's, and his body, shape, and feet like an eagle, and that he can take up a moose with one of his claws."[6]

Leroy Dudley

The yarns of Leroy Dudley about Pamola have been catalogued in the book, *"Chimney Pond Tales."*

At the end of the 1991 edition of that book, in the section, "Things to Read About Katahdin," the authors note the essay by Fannie Hardy Eckstorm, printed in 1924 on the basic Pamola story, "is where Dudley took off from." This is not to say Dudley read Eckstorm's piece, rather, the stories Mrs. Eckstorm includes in her writing, were similar to the stories Leroy Dudley heard over his lifetime spent in the woods, and from his family.

Leroy Dudley was born in 1873 (or 1874) and was a guide at Mount Katahdin from the 1890s until his death in 1942. Leroy Dudley's father, Mark Dudley was a

---

[6] History of Maine, by W. D. Williamson. Vol. 1, p. 92, (ed. 1832).

woodsman and is said to have had a long friendship with the Governor of the Penobscot Indians, John Neptune. Neptune was a trapper and was a friend of Manly Hardy (Mrs. Eckstorm's father), who was a well-known trapper and Maine woodsman.

It has been said that Leroy Dudley's grandfather was also friends with John Neptune. And so it suspected that many of the stories have been handed down generation to generation.

"Chimney Pond Tales," is a book assembled by Clayton and Jane Thomas with Elizabeth Hall Harmon of Leroy Dudley's Pamola yarns. Published by The Pamola Press, Cumberland Center, Maine (1991).

I should question that statement of "head and face like a man's," if, as seems most likely, this great bird is the same as the Passamaquoddy *Culloo*. The Indian drawing in Leland's *Algonquin Legends* shows the Culloo with the head and beak of an eagle. What we can gather with certainty is that some huge bird was supposed to live upon Katahdin. That this was a Culloo seems probable from the following very ancient Indian tale related by John Gyles, the interpreter, in his account of his captivity between 1689 and 1698:

The first, of a Boy who was carried away by a large Bird called a Gulloua, who buildeth her Nest on a high Rock or Mountain. A Boy was Hunting with his Bow & Arrow at the foot of a Rocky Mountain, when the

Gulloua came diving thro' the Air, grasp'd the Boy in her Talons; and tho' he was eight or ten Years of Age, she soar'd aloft, and laid him in her Nest, a Prey for her Young; where the Boy lay constantly on his Face, but would look sometimes under his Arms and saw two Young Ones with much Fish and Flesh in the Nest, and the old Bird constantly bringing more. So that the young Ones not touching him, the old One claw'd him up and set him where she found him; who returned, and related the odd Event to his Friends. As I have, in a Canoe, pass'd near the Mountain, the Indians have said to me, There is the Nest of the great Bird that carried the Boy away: And there seem'd to be a great number of Sticks put together in form of a Nest on the Top of the Mountain. At another time they said, There is the Bird, but he is now as a Boy to a Giant, to what he was in former Days. The Bird which they pointed to was a large speckled Bird, like an Eagle, tho' somewhat larger.[7]

The bird Gyles saw was unquestionably a golden eagle. We may assume that this bird was the prototype of the dreaded Culloo. While it would be too much to say that the Maliseet Culloo was the same as the Penobscot Storm-bird of Katahdin,

---

[7] *Memoirs of Odd Adventures, Strange Deliverances, etc., in the Captivity of John Gyles, Esq.* (Boston, 1736), chap. 5, p. 23. I am indebted to Mr. Lawrence C. Wroth, the librarian of the John Carter Brown Library, Providence, R. I., for these extracts from the original edition of Gyles's Captitity. It has been reprinted by Drake, in his *Book of the Indian*, and separately, in 1869, in Cincinnati, but both are inferior versions.

the resemblance is striking. It is, however, not to be confounded with *Wuchowsen*, the Wind-bird, that by the flapping of its wings makes the breezes.

The picture of Pamola, several times reproduced from Vetromile's book, excludes the conception of this Storm-bird, as it has no wings. But it mingles the other two. Vetromile's Pamola is a giant, with huge limbs, but a very short body, and with very long hair; he is armed with a bow and wears a quiver on his shoulder. The sketch has not a vestige of authority. It must have been done from description by someone hired by the New York publishers. No better is Vetromile's explanation of the word "Pamola" as, "he curses on the mountain," since it has no root which seems to mean "curses" and none which can possibly mean "mountain."

Vetromile's 1866 Depiction of Pamola.

The only Indian representation of Pamola that I know is the mark affixed as signature to a letter, written in 1784 by six Penobscot chiefs. The signatures are reproduced in facsimile in the *Centennial History of Orono, Maine*, but the explanatory text blunders badly when it says that the signature of Pierre Sock is Pamola and that of Arexes (Alexis) is Machehantu, the Devil. It is Alexis who signs with Pamola, and has drawn a large-headed, eared creature, with big eyes, with a single line standing for both head and body and with crooked lines for legs and arms. It has neither wings nor talons, but has a sort of impish, futile malevolence about it, corresponding well to old Clara Neptune's idea of Pamola already quoted. Once she told me, "Bahmolai go round yet; once in while you hear um; no hurt." This agrees with what an Indian told my father seventy years ago: "How we know Bahmolai there on Katahdin when can't seen um? - *Hear um!* He go *oo-oo-oooh* over top of gun-barrel!" Clearly enough this is nothing but the wind; and this is what the Indian means when speaking of Bumole to other Indians.

Orono Centennial Celebration

The following is a copy of the facsimile of the signature marks contained in the, *"Centennial Celebration and Dedication of Town Hall, Orono, Maine, March 3, 1874,"* as referenced by Eckstorm. The marks are labeled, *"Signatures Of Tarratine Chiefs Mentioned by Judge Godfrey, Nov. 22, 1775."* Also included is the original text that accompanied the marks.

The correction to which mark is really meant to be a depiction of Pamola was clarified by Eckstorm in the text and is represented as this image.

Original Text, (*uncorrected*):

Orono subscribed his mark, which was a fac-simile of the seal; Nextambawit's was that of a lynx; Josephsus's, that of a large silver brooch; Alsonsa's, of two stone implements crossed; Nexteumet's, of a terrapin; Pierre Sock's, of Pomola, perhaps [the spirit of Katahdin]; Arexes's of, it may be, Majahundi [the devil].

* See Eckstorm text that Arexes's mark is that of Pamola. Names have been re-typed on this image for clarity, although the image spelling of *Nextambawit varies from the text.*

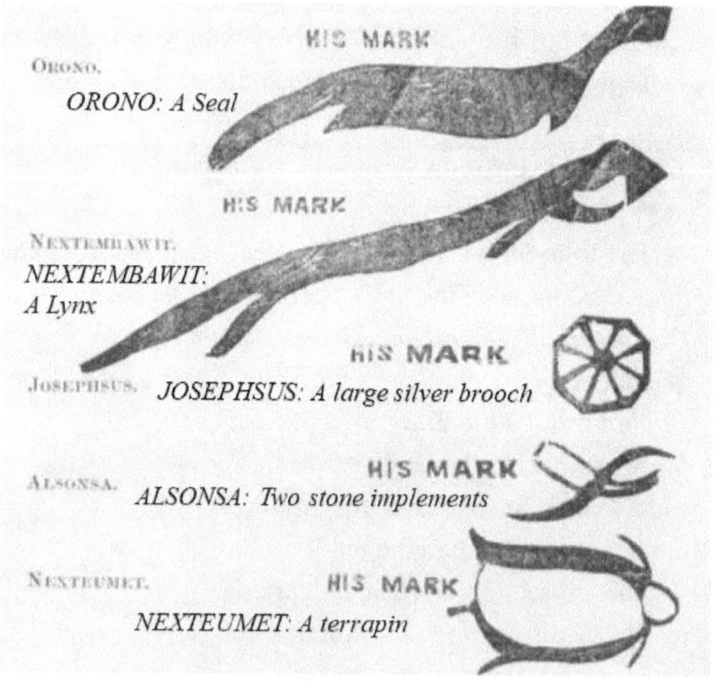

ORONO, ORONO: A Seal

NEXTEMBAWIT. NEXTEMBAWIT: A Lynx

JOSEPHSUS. JOSEPHSUS: A large silver brooch

ALSONSA. ALSONSA: Two stone implements

NEXTEUMET. NEXTEUMET: A terrapin

Not mentioned by Eckstorm in this essay, but noted elsewhere in her writings she remarked the labels for Orono and Nextembawit are also incorrect. Orono's mark was,

'The Beaver;' and she clarified, "no Indian would draw a seal with the hind feet separate from a long, broad tail." Likewise, Nextembawit's mark was a mink, fox, or otter, but most likely, 'The Squirrel;' for "what Indian would represent a long-legged, short-tailed animal like a lynx as having short legs and a long tail?"

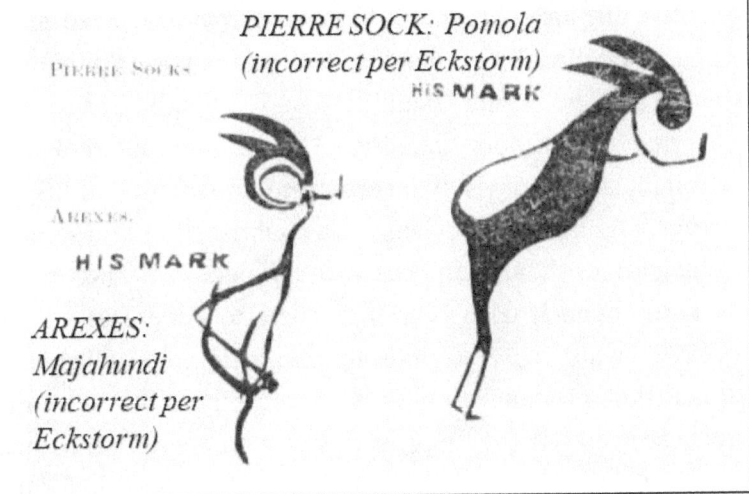

PIERRE SOCK: Pomola (incorrect per Eckstorm)

AREXES: Majahundi (incorrect per Eckstorm)

The giant who lives inside the mountain is entirely different. They seem to identify him with the thunder and lightning, of which, oddly enough, Indians are little afraid. I have found indications that one prominent Indian family regards itself as descended from the Thunder, most likely through the Indian girl who was carried off; but the evidence gathered is not conclusive. At least this being is human in shape and feelings. As old Clara said: "Katahdin, he man." He is beautiful in body, of majestic appearance, not a surly, misshapen giant. I have never heard for him any name but "Katahdin," which is not his name.

Katahdin is simply "The Big Hill," from *keght*, or *k't*, big, or principal, and the inseparable *-adene*, mountain. Gyles and

Turner, writing before 1804, use it, though not invariably, with the definite article, showing that they understood the Indian, and Moses Greenleaf, in 1829, also speaks of it as "the Katahdin." The various forms of the word differ more in looks than in sound. Gyles's "Teddon" is good Indian and contains both roots, though *k't* is shortened to the final letter and *adn* is a little disguised. Turner's "Catardin" is pronounced exactly like Katahdin; for no Yankee will pronounce an *r* if he can avoid it. The forms "Natardin" and "Notadn," assigned to Turner, are without standing. They are his attempt at the pronunciation, unwisely incorporated into the title of his letter describing his ascent when it was published by a friend. The much affected "Ktaadn" has a similar pedigree. The first time I have found it used is in a footnote to Greenleaf's Survey (1829), where he gives it as approximating the Indian sound; "but this pronunciation is next to impossible for organs accustomed only to English; it is written, therefore, in such a manner as will most naturally express in English form the nearest approximation of the Indian word" — that is, as "Katahdin."

The first mention of Katahdin, in Gyles's *Captivity*, published in 1736, is a lovely bit of English prose, as limpid and bright flowing as Katahdin Brook:

I have heard an Indian say that he lived by the River at the Foot of the *Teddon*, and in his Wigwam, seeing the top of it thro' the Hole left in the top of the Wigwam for the passing of Smoke, he was tempted to travel to it: accordingly he set out early on a Summer's Morning, and laboured hard in ascending the Hill all Day, and the Top seem'd as distant from the Place where he lodged at Night, as from the Wigwam whence he began his Journey; and concluding that Spirits were there, never dare make a second Attempt.

He goes on:

I have been credibly inform'd that several others have fail'd in the same Attempt: particularly, that three young Men towr'd the *Teddon* three days and an half, and then began to be strangely disorder'd & delirious, and when their Imagination was clear, and they could recollect where they were, and had been, they found themselves return'd one Days Journey: how they came down so far, they can't guess, unless the Genii of the Place convey'd them!

The traditions recorded by Gyles go back in written form two hundred years; for he says that his manuscript lay by him "for some years" before it was printed in 1736. There is nothing else so valuable, both by reason of its age and because Gyles was as well qualified as any Indian to give an understanding version of the tales.

The next reference to Katahdin is not by its familiar name. In 1764, John Chadwick, the surveyor, going up the Penobscot to Quebec passed the mountain and evidently climbed part way up the southern side. He calls it "Satinhungermoss Hill," which must mean "Nesowadnehunk-lake Hill," and says in part:

(It is) a remarkable Hill for height and figure. The Indians say that this Hill is the highest in the country; that "they" can ascend so high as any green grows and no higher; that one Indian attempted to go higher but he never returned.[8]

August 13, 1804, Charles Turner, Jr., with six men from Bangor and Orono and two Indians, made the first recorded ascent of the mountain. This has been reprinted in part in APPALACHIA, and entire in other places.[9]

Of the legend Turner says:

The Indians have a superstition respecting this mountain, that an evil spirit, whom they call Pamola, inhabits it, at least in the winter, and flies off in the spring with tremendous rumbling noises. They have a tradition that no person, i.e., native, who has attempted to ascend it, has lived to return. They allege that, many moons ago, seven Indians resolutely ascended the mountain and that they never were heard of afterwards, having undoubtedly been killed by Pamola in the mountain. The two Indians whom we hired to pilot and assist us in ascending the mountain, cautioned us not to proceed if we should hear any uncommon noise; and when we came to the cold part of the mountain they refused to proceed ahead - however,

---

[8] Bangor Historical Magazine, Vol. IV (1888-89), p. 146.
[9] *APPALACHIA*, Vol. 13 (May, 1913), "Early American Mountaineers," by Allen H. Bent. Also, Mass. Hist. Colls., 2d Series, Vol. 8, and Sprague's Journal of Maine History, Vol. 10, No. 3 (1922).

when they found that we were determined to proceed even without them, they went forward courageously, and seemed ambitious to be first on the summit. On our return to Indian Oldtown, it was with difficulty that we could convince the natives that we had been upon the top of Mount Catardin, nor should we have been able to satisfy them of the fact, so superstitious were they, had it not been for the Indians who accompanied us.

We notice here that Pamola is represented as winged and as living there in winter only, and that, instead of being turned back by the spirits, venturesome men disappear forever. Even among the Indians the legend seems to have changed in the century since Gyles heard it. Judge Williamson, in 1832, recorded a belief among the Indians in this same Storm-spirit; and in 1837, when Dr. Charles T. Jackson was caught on the top in a severe northeast snowstorm, his Indian, Louis Neptune, "declared that Pamola was angry with us for pretending to measure the height of the mountain and revenged himself upon us by this storm." Gyles, Chadwick, Turner, Williamson, Jackson and Keep, the only ones who left any record, before 1850, of an unseen power inhabiting Katahdin, all agree that it is harmful only to those who ascend the mountain top; "as far as any green grows," they were safe. Clearly it was a wind spirit that they feared. The spirit inside the mountain was different.

Before passing to the tales of this other being, or beings, we should note that it was not Katahdin alone that the Indians were afraid of. They feared to ascend any high mountain.

When Darby Field, of Exeter, made the first ascent of Mount Washington, June, 1642, Winthrop[10] says that when they were within eight miles of the top, the Indians told him "that no Indian ever dared to go higher, and that he would die if he went." It is in John Josselyn's books that we get a clue to the reason. That Josselyn made the ascent, not with Field, as Belknap unguardedly states, but on his second visit, probably after 1668, we infer from the vividness of his description of the view from Mount Washington, over a country "daunting terrible, full of rocky Hills as thick as Mole-hills in a Meadow, and cloathed with Infinite thick Woods." In the *Two Voyages* he says: "Some suppose that the White Mountains were first raised by Earthquakes, *they are hollow* as may be guessed by the resounding of the rain upon the level on the top." Who that had not heard for himself the clinking hollowness of the frost-riven leaves of granite upon our New England hills, would ever have said that? Then he tells how the Indians had told him of an earthquake in the White Mountains in 1668, and how among the French an earthquake had rent "a huge Rock asunder even to the center, wherein was a vast hollow of an immeasurable depth, out of which came many infernal Spirits." The Indians had been telling Josselyn of their superstitions, and he checks it up by his own reason for believing that the mountains were hollow, mere bubbles blown up by earthquakes; and if hollow, why not the abode of evil spirits, as the Indians said? In short, the notion of spirits inside the mountains was not peculiar to Katahdin. These big, lone hills were wigwams, like their own, the abode of giants, people

---

[10] History of New England, Vol. 11, pp. 67, 68, 88 (Savage edition). [No year given on original footnote.]

not unlike themselves. "All mountain have Injun in um," said Old Clara; "live there in mountain."

But in one respect these beings were unlike men; they all had eyebrows of stone, and their cheekbones were stony. The belief was general. David Cusick, an Iroquois, writing in 1825, telling of the same belief among his own people, aptly names these "the stonish men." He said that Sir William Johnson had a picture of one of them in his home — no doubt a man in armor; and Robert W. Chambers, in *The Maid-at-Arms,* makes effective use of the remark.

There are two main themes of this Katahdin myth — one of the girl who married Katahdin, the other of the hunter who went into the mountain and married the daughter of the old man who lives there. As I have seen only Passamaquoddy (that is, Maliseet) versions of the latter, it is enough to say that Leland gives the story.

Of the other tale I have found five different versions — three Penobscot, one Maliseet, and Gyles's very early and highly authentic rendering, which is probably Maliseet, though most likely first heard when he was near the mountain. He says:

There is an old Story told among the Indians of a Family, who had a Daughter that was accounted a finished Beauty, and adorned with the precious Jewel of an Indian Education! So form'd by Nature and polish'd by Art they could not find for her a suitable Consort! At length, while they resided on the Head of Penobscot River, under the White-Hills called the *Teddon*, this fine Creature was missing; and her Parents could have no Account of her. After much Time spent, Pains, and Tears show'red in quest of her; they saw her, diverting herself with a beautiful Youth, whose Hair like her's flow'd down below his Waist, Swimming, Washing, & in the Water; but the Youths vanished upon their Approach. This beautiful Person, whom they imagin'd to be one of those kind Spirits who inhabit the Teddon; they look'd upon him as their Son-in-Law: so that (according to Custom) they called upon him for Moose, Bear, or whatever Creature they desired, and if they did but go to the Water-side and signify their desire, the Creature which they would have, came Swimming to them![11]

There is no need to repeat Vetromile's version, which is inferior. Leland's was given him by Maria Sakis, a Penobscot woman, and runs thus:

Of the old time. There was once an Indian girl gathering blueberries on Mount Katahdin. And, being lonely, she said, "I would that I had a husband!" And seeing the great mountain in all its glory rising on high, with the red sunlight on the top, she added, "I wish Katahdin were a man, and would marry me!"

All this she was heard to say ere she went onward and up the mountain, but for three years she was never seen again. Then she reappeared, bearing a babe, a beautiful child, but his little eyebrows were of stone. For the Spirit

---

[11] Memoirs of Odd Adventures, etc. (Boston, 1736), p. 29. From the original by courtesy of John Carter Brown Library.

of the Mountain had taken her to himself; and when she greatly desired to return to her own people, he told her to go in peace, but forbade her to tell any man who had married her.

Now the boy had strange gifts, and the wise men said that he was born to become a mighty magician. For when he did but point his finger at a moose, or anything which ran, it would drop dead; and when in a canoe, if he pointed at the flocks of wild ducks or swans, then the water was at once covered with the floating game, and they gathered them in as they listed, and through that boy his mother and everyone had food and to spare.

Now this was the truth, and it was a great wonder, that Katahdin had wedded this girl, thinking with himself and his wife to bring up a child who should build up his nation, and make of the Wabanaki a mighty race. And he said, "Declare unto these people that they are not to inquire of thee who is the father of thy child; truly they will all know it by seeing him, for they shall not grieve thee with impertinence." Now the woman had made it known that she would not be questioned, and she gave them all what they needed; yet, for all this they could not restrain themselves from talking to her on what they well knew she would fain be silent. And one day when they had angered her, she thought, "Truly Katahdin was right; these people are in no wise worthy of my son, neither shall he serve them; he shall not lead them to victory; they are not of those who make a great nation." And being still further teased and tormented, she spake[12] and said: "Ye fools,

---

[12] Archaic past tense of speak.

who by your own folly will kill yourselves; ye mud-wasps, who sting the fingers which would pick ye out of the water, why will ye ever trouble me to tell you what you well know? Can you not see who was the father of my boy? Behold his eyebrows; do ye not know Katahdin by them? But it shall be to your exceeding great sorrow that ever ye inquired. From this day ye may feed yourselves and find your own venison, for this child shall do so no more for you."

And she arose and went her way into the woods and up the mountain, and was seen on earth no more.[13]

The following is the version told Miss Minnie Atkinson, in the presence of Mr. Wallace Brown, the Indian agent, by a member of the Passamaquoddy tribe:

Once there was a girl who was called Red Rose. She was very beautiful. One day she wandered in the woods a long way from home. At length she came to a place from which she could see Mount Katahdin. As she looked at it she wished that she could have a husband as big and strong as the mountain. She had walked a very long way, and she was very tired. So while she thought of the husband she would like to have, she sat down by the foot of a tree, and presently she fell asleep. When she awoke there was an immense Indian standing before her.

"I am the Spirit of Katahdin," he said. "I know your wish. I have come to marry you."

---

[13] Algonquin Legends of New England, by C. G. Leland (Boston, 1884), p. 255.

He asked her to go to the mountain with him. It was a very long way.

"I cannot walk so far," she said.

"I did not ask you to walk," he answered. "I will carry you."

So he set her upon his shoulder, and went away with her to Katahdin. The entrance to the mountain was in its side between some rocks where it could not easily be found. The Spirit of Katahdin took her within the mountain, past the rocks, and there she dwelt with him most happily.

By and by a little boy and a little girl were born. As the years passed, however, Red Rose began to grow homesick.

"I wish I could go home," she said one day.

"You shall have your wish," answered the Spirit of Katahdin. He gave her some medicine that made her once more young and beautiful. As a parting gift he said that whenever the girl passed her hand over her lips her words should come true, and that at whatever the boy pointed a finger it should die.

So Red Rose went home to her tribe by the great waters of the Passamaquoddy Bay. She took with her the little girl and the little boy. When they reached home it was a time of famine. There was nothing to eat in the wigwams; there was no game in the woods; there were no fish in the bay nor in the river and lakes. Everybody was sad. Red Rose felt sad also, but the little girl passed her hand over her mouth and said that there was game in the woods. At once the woods were full of game. The little boy pointed his finger at a deer, and it fell dead. Then he pointed at a moose, and that fell dead. He happened to point at an

Indian, and he too fell dead. The little girl passed her hand over her mouth and said that all the lakes and rivers were full of eels. Then they were full of eels, and there was a great deal to eat. Everybody was happy, and there was no more famine.

The story goes on, briefly telling how Red Rose helped her people to fight the Micmacs, and in closing says that every hundred years Red Rose comes back to visit the tribe, "and she is very, very beautiful indeed."

It is said among the Indians that many present grandparents saw Red Rose when she came on the last century visit. For a long time, Indians were afraid — some are still — to go up to the top of Mount Katahdin lest they meet the Spirit of the Mountain who dwells in its heart beyond the secret stone portal.[14]

This last version is one that I took down myself from Mrs. Clara Neptune, a very old Penobscot woman. Four times, in different years, she told me the story, both in Indian and in English, and this is blended from her different accounts. Each time she held to the main theme, which differs from all the other versions in that the girl does not wish to marry Katahdin.

"Ev'ry mountain got Injun in it. Katahdin, he man; mountain once was man." She went on to tell about a girl who used to live at Oldtown, a beautiful girl and a great

---

[14] Hinckley Township, or Grand Lake Stream Plantation, by Minnie Atkinson (Newburyport, Mass., 1920), pp. 121, 122.

belle. "Name? - Don't know it her name. No, not chief's daughter - just girl."

All the young men courted her. "Used be anybody want girl, used take waubub (wampum) his folks. Young men all bring it bunches beads his folks; but dis girl don't want it anybody 'tall. Good many fellows want her, couldn't got her.

"One time dancin' 'mong rocks, singin', singin':

" 'Ef he was man, Katahdin,

I wouldn' marry um;

I wouldn' marry no man dis world.' "

Each time the Old Lady varied the little song. "Got pretty tune," she said; "used sing it that song myself."

Once she gave it in Indian, and the translation is her own.

> Mothgehbeh Katahdinosis
> (Ef he was Katahdin)
> Chewl medeh dahabah
> (He wanted to marry me)
> Nisweeoowaynewah
> (I wouldn't marry him.)

"Den come Katahdin. Somebody he's standin' near his back, he seize um, carry um off." She was taken to Katahdin's home inside the mountain; for the mountain is all hollow inside. "Had it good wigwam-camp inside; big tent; boughs; everyding; moosemeat; bluebellies. Katahdin he's got father, mother, folks, everythin'. Dat ooman he don' want nothin' victuals."

There she lived and in time was born little Katahdinosis, with the stony eyebrows. But Katahdin was away much of the time and the young mother longed to see her own father and mother and to show them her baby. "Pecheelun Katahdin macheepan katahdinook sekahden oudichlun: 'Kateh nahmehan comeetahwoos keegahwoos.' Katahdin he told um: You want gone seen you folks, you can gone seen um father, mother. You take um baby.'

"Den he carry his wife one day. 'You go see father, mother. Only leetle boy, don' make him bow-arrow. When he see anythin' he p'int. Don' you let him anythin' danger - no bow-arrow; no knife.'"

But the old man is so pleased with his grandson that he wants to amuse the child. "Dis ol' man when he see his daughter, dat leetle boy — (he got rock here - eyebrows) — he set down outdoors, make um bow-arrow his grandson. First thing he kill his grandfadder. 'Fore dat he only p'int at bird, at deer, moose-kill um. Used be when he see bird flyin' he p'int at birds" — (laying one forefinger over the other, crooked like a bow) — "p'int with finger like bow 'n arrow, and birds come down. Now kill grandpa.

"Den dat night he come get um Katahdin.

"Dat's what make um Injuns down dere — (in Katahdin). Mus' be good many of 'em dere now. Joe Flances his camp Debsconeag, he can hear it gun, fiddle, hear um play bowl on mountain, hear hloot (flute), see light in mountain. All livin' now in mountain, livin' in Katahdin."

And she bent forward, intent as if listening to hear the magic flutes that you can hear at Joe Frances's camp on Debsconeag.

No one can say that any one of these versions is right and the others wrong. Perhaps they all come from the same long story, broken down by time into incidents; perhaps they are individual variations through family tradition or personal choice. But we observe that in each there is the selection of detail which makes it consistent and artistic, and it would be a mistake for anyone now to try to combine the versions into one more complete. In one point all agree: not one names the hero of it — to all he is just Katahdin, "the Big Hill."

These are the legends of Katahdin — the wind, Pamola; the Storm-bird, who hovers round its summit in winter; the Spirit of Katahdin, like a man in his life and loves, who, with his household, dwells inside it.

— Fannie Pearson Hardy

Note: Eckstorm purposely did not edit Clara Neptune's words or pronunciations. While this may make the story a little more challenging to read, this was Eckstorm's typical method to keep the facts original to the source.

Old Advertisement for a Sporting Camp.

IV — The Swan's Road To Katahdin

by
Anna Boynton Averill

Sailing through soft, mid-summer hours, we go
The "Swan's road to Katahdin." Lakes and streams
Break the deep woods with shining paths that flow
From thee to me, O, mountain of my dreams!

The far Northeast, thy shadowy realm of snows,
Was part of Heaven for me in days long flown,
And thou — when after storm thy form arose,
Majestic, glorious — wast the great White Throne.

As this dream melted like the morning's breath,
The Indian hunter to our hearth would come
With legends of a spirit dark as death,
Who made thy lone and hoary height his home.

But the glad years have brought me one by one,
Dreams that come true. Before the boat, hope flies
To thy fair altar shining in the sun . . .
— O, that thine high priest were a poet wise!

That there might be unblemished offerings,
Worship embalmed in song's ambrosial wine,
Upborne to thee on bright, immortal wings,
And poured upon thy pure, supernal shrine.

. . . How wilt thou welcome us, O, lonely king?
— Thy royal promise for a king is meet.
Thou wilt uphold us in the clouds and bring
Thy wild and lovely kingdom to our feet.

The mention of the "Swan's road to Katahdin" was a saying referring to going towards Katahdin by way of the Penobscot River.

The following is half of an 1870s stereograph image by A.L. Hinds. It is labeled,
"By the Swan's Road to Katahdin"

V — Windbound On Chamberlain

Forest and Stream – November 7, 1889

IT used to be the custom of the old cartographers to leave no blank space on their maps; and when their geographical knowledge gave out, they filled the unexplored regions with pictures symbolical of the dangers supposed to be lurking in those wilds — lions and unicorns, dragons, griffins, wyverns, statant, couchant, saltant, rampant, guardant, saliant— neither the animals nor their attitudes being calculated to soothe the apprehensions of the adventurous. In like manner we today imagine that the woods are full of wild creatures, yet when I reviewed my woods notes to find some red-letter day full of the birds and their doings, I could not think of one which compared with many spent in field and hedgerow. There are few birds in the woods.

The wilderness is a wilderness indeed, barren of life; and you can find more birds, more plants and more game within five miles of settlements, than in an equal space of forest. As Thoreau says:

"Generally speaking, a howling wilderness
does not howl; it is the imagination of the traveler
that does the howling."

Since I cannot find a day which is at all noteworthy for the observations it afforded, something prompts me to select one which was wholly ordinary, and yet pleasant to remember; that day when, having crossed Mud Pond Carry, we camped on the side of Chamberlain.

Those who remember the "boundary dispute" of 1842 may locate this lake, on being told that it lies just north of the highland which the English claimed, the Dutch Commissioners debated upon, and Col. Graham surveyed, as the northeastern boundary of the United States, said "highlands" being Mud Pond Carry et al. Those who know the country best concede great credit to Col. Graham's ability in his survey, not only for discovering that the land here is high, but that there is any visible above water.

Mud Pond Carry is the most famous road in the State. Thoreau says of it, with a pun on one of our lumbermen's terms, "This was the most perfectly swamped of all the roads I ever saw;" but the remark is lacking in originality to those who have seen the place. Mud Pond Carry leads to Mud Pond, and Mud Pond outlets into Chamberlain Lake, the largest lake in Maine as a tributary to the St. John.

We were belated in crossing the carry, and we delayed a little paddling across Mud Pond, for after a week of rain this morning seemed doubly fine, and the view of Katahdin — grand old Katahdin — lacking nothing of being a perfect mountain, and as savage today as when Leif Erickson landed,[15] was so glorious that we could not resist it. Then there was half a mile of quick water at the outlet, where the canoe had to be "waded" down, while the passengers went overland by the

---

[15] Leif Erikson (c. 970 – c. 1020) [also as, Leiv Eiriksson or Leif Ericson] was a Norse explorer from Iceland. It is thought he may have been the first known European to have set foot on continental North America.

carry until they reached the meadows, where they (the passengers aforesaid) stood on stumps in order to keep out of the water, and surveyed the wide, green meadows, fair in color, but desolate to look on, because of the standing dead trees, killed by the flowage, until the canoe came down. Then there was a short voyage through the meadows, past newly-built muskrat houses. At one place the wind brought down the smell of tainted meat — some moose or caribou which had been left to spoil. All these delays consumed valuable time, and meanwhile the wind had risen as we had feared it would, when we were so hindered in crossing the carry. When at last the lake was reached, such a sea was running that it was deemed imprudent to attempt to cross.

Chamberlain Lake is twelve miles long by two to three miles wide and has the name of being a *very ugly lake*, which in woods parlance is equivalent to *dangerous*. It lies over 900 feet above the sea, extended from northwest to southeast, without an island in it capable of affording any shelter, and not only exposed to all the winds, but subject to draughts which raise a cross and choppy sea. It is also distinguished by having two inlets and two outlets, one of them artificial. It is not a beautiful lake.

There is no high land near it, and the shores, which are straight and forbidding, are even to this day fenced with the trees killed by the flowage when the locks were built nearly fifty years ago. The locks, about which a word should be said, are at the natural outlet — two dams with a space between them, built for the purpose of driving the logs cut on the lower lake, which naturally would go down the St. John, up into

Chamberlain, thence through Telosinis[16] and Telos, and down the artificial "cut" into the Penobscot. The locks having nothing to do with navigation, no boat larger that a batteau ever floated on Chamberlain.

We held the canoe in the Mud Brook inlet for a time, and looked at the heavy sea which was running outside; listened to the doleful creaking of the dead wood as the waves sawed one long tree against another, and subsiding showed ugly black snags sticking out, on which a canoe would be wrecked instantly; looked again at the farm opposite, and reluctantly drew back. Experience, in one of her hardest lessons, had taught one of the party not to dare Chamberlain needlessly. As we turned, we saw some small duck dipping and feeding among the driftwood, but just as the gun was pointed at him he saved himself by diving. One may be a strict bird defender at home, but in the woods everything goes to fill the kettle.

We were more easily consoled for our failure to cross, because it was dinner time. We managed with some difficulty to get ashore on the right side of the stream, in a growth of sapling birch and poplar; and, fortunately, remembered to build our fire where the smoke would not attract the attention of the men at the farm. For now, as in Thoreau's day, a smoke near the inlet is a signal for the farm to send a canoe across, some two miles and a half. Even in their great sea canoes this

---

[16] As noted on the map by Hubbard as Telosinis, or Pataquongamis. See, Woods and Lakes of Maine, and Hubbard's Guide to Moosehead Lake and Northern Maine. Now renamed, unimaginatively, to Round Pond.

would have been no easy task on such a day. (Mr. Coe,[17] the owner of the farm, tells me that in winter they always leave a lamp burning all night, to guide any wandering lumberman belated on the lake.)

Dinner is not an elaborate meal in the woods. Ours was soon finished, and we had the afternoon before us; for evidently we were windbound. "And yet the wind might go down," we said, watching the treetops bend, and knowing very well that there was no such happiness in store. How beautiful across the angry lake the farm looked, seated on the sloping hillside among fields colored with the soft rich hues of growing grain, of grassland and of cultivated soil. Not one of the other "supply" farms compares with this in picturesqueness, as seen across the lake.

These great farms are a surprise to strangers. Here is Chamberlain, some 80 miles from the nearest railroad, and 60 from the nearest main road, one of the only two houses on a block of twenty-eight townships — a space larger than the State of Rhode Island. What can be done with the produce of these hundreds of acres? It is all for the winter's business. For fifty years this farm has raised hay and grain for the lumbermen's cattle, and potatoes for the men themselves. It is too cold here to ripen maize, although at Trout Brook Farm, 30 miles to the east, a little is grown. A few staple vegetables are raised, and these, with the large quantities of grain and hay, are the objects of the farm's existence.

---

[17] Background on Chamberlain Farm and E. S. Coe, who was part owner of the supply farm with David Pingree, has been provided in, *Canoe and Camera – A Two Hundred Mile Tour Through The Maine Forests - Annotated Edition*, by Tommy Carbone (Burnt Jackey Publishing, 2021).

While we were thus forced to lie still, there was a good opportunity given to watch the birds; but except for a kingfisher which sat on the other side of the stream, and some impudent Canada jays which came ca-ca-ca-ing about, I saw nothing. The jays tiptoed about on the trees, bowing and bending; they fluttered down with spread wings and tails, and made themselves such nuisances, that until one of them came under the scalpel of the taxidermist there was no peace to be had. I should not omit from the list of birds two partridges, which made an excellent stew a little later, and a herring gull which sat on a rock in the lake about 200 yards off, and was saved only by the ball falling a little short of him.

These large lakes are close reproductions of the seashore, even to the sea gulls which breed here, although they are never seen between the lower end of Moosehead and salt water. It would be unkind not to mention the beautiful green caterpillar that lived on a poplar nearby, so strong, so firm in his muscles, so silken skinned, and so intelligent in his determination to go to the place he had in mind, that I remember him with pleasure. But, except a dish of raspberries, that was all that the woods had for us. What city garden would not have yielded more in half a day?

The wind did not abate as we had hoped; so, at last, the tent was pitched on the same spot where someone else had been windbound before us. But the afternoon had not passed unpleasantly; it was too great a treat to see blue sky above us, after our rainy week, to demur at having to wait for the wind. And, then, we had resolved to get up before the wind the next morning.

That night a woods mouse came into the tent and hopped over me, tapping my face softly. Camping out sometimes gives one strange bedfellows — toads, lizards, bats, flying squirrels, and mice to wit; but it is all part of the fun.

The next morning our first call came at 2 A.M., but this was reconsidered, and for two hours more we were allowed to sleep. Then a hasty toilet in the dark, a cold bite, and the tent was struck, the baggage packed, the canoe loaded, and we were off before daylight. The lake was smooth as glass; yesterday's swell was lost in the calm which on fresh water follows so quickly on the subsidence of the wind. Off in the east a red line pierced the gloom, and spread until it lighted all the heavens on that side with fiery, vermilion-tinted hues, leaving the treetops black and jagged as the walls of a burning building. Overhead flew a young herring gull, and he, too, looked black in this morning conflagration.

And now the water began to curdle like hot milk. Before the sun was fairly up the wind began to ripple over the surface of the water, gathering force as it went, which was in a direction opposite to that from which the curdle came. The wind was up, the waves rolled and broke, but we were across Chamberlain.

— Fannie Pearson Hardy

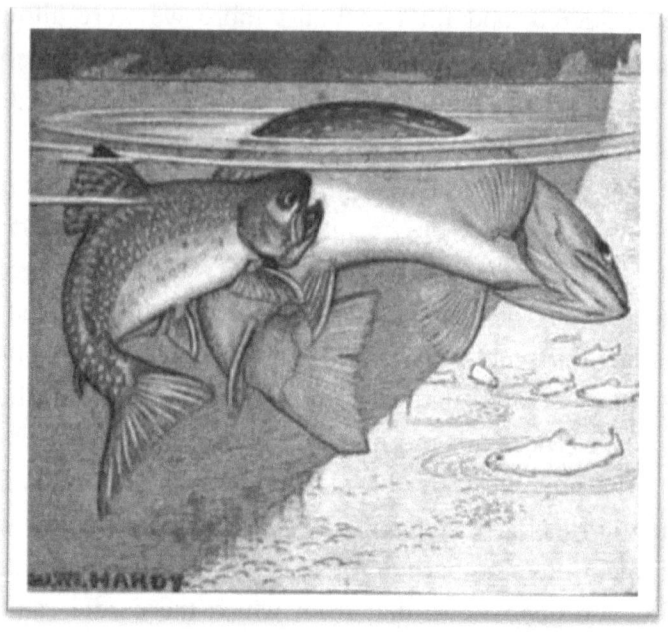

Illustration by Walter M. Hardy

VI — Camp Solitude

by
Anna Boynton Averill

The Spirit of the summer wilds
   Sent down the day by breeze and bird,
   A summons that our sad hearts heard,
(She soothes all sorrow with her smiles.)

And so we sought the sylvan shore
   And healing waters still and lone,
   That whisper of the loved and gone
Who seek with us these haunts no more.

Beside the lake they loved so well,
   With plumy woods on either hand,
   On a green bluff above the sand
We pitched our tent and here we dwell.

Here, points and islands wooded deep,
   Below us, eastward softly break
   The low blue waters of the lake
In coves and pools where shadows sleep.

The woods go north, far, green and dark,
   O'er deep ravines and vales and hills.
   At morn we trace their hidden rills
By mists that rise their course to mark.

Southward we hear, at break of day,
   The cocks crow on the distant farms;
   The hound's deep bay wakes far alarms,
And cow bells tinkle as they stray.

At noon the partridge beats tattoo;
   At dead of night when winds are rough,
   The loons sail up below the bluff,
And wake us with their wild halloo.

From out the dells the chickadee
   Comes forth to share our evening meal;
   The gull and fish hawk dip and wheel,
And blue jays call from cliff and tree.

From morn till eve the cricket sings;
   The fairest brook our eyes have seen
   Comes murmuring down the dim ravine,
And to the lake its treasure brings.

And sky and water change like dreams.
   Sometimes below our little boat
   The cloud-strewn blue is seen to float,
Sometimes a sunset glory streams.

Across the waters and they take
   The rose and gold and purple on;
   Again the tender hues of dawn
Flow down and fill the dreaming lake.

And shower and storm and wind come o'er
   The northern hills, by turns, and break
   The waters into foam and shake
The shores and set the woods aroar.

And then, in breezy days of sun,
   We lie for hours upon the steep
   And watch the great cloud shadows sweep
The hills and down the waters run.

This is the land of Afternoon;
   The golden hours bring time for thought;
   With rest, and peace, and meaning fraught,
We take them as a precious boon.

Here talk, nor toil, nor cares intrude.
   On the calm tide we float and dream,
   Down drifting gently with the stream,
Through the sweet haunts of solitude.

Sweet Haunts of Solitude
(Editor's Collection)

VII — "Going to Mount Katahdin"

FOR two centuries Katahdin has been beckoning climbers, the legends of Pamola only a deterrent to a few. In the beginning, parties to climb the mountain often left their names in vials for others to find. On returning, accounts of their climb appeared in the papers. Sometimes, unlike Thoreau's journal, these accounts were written anonymously or signed with only initials, making identification a process of historical discovery. In, *Exploring the Maine Woods – The Hardy Family Expedition to the Machias Lakes,* an excerpt of a letter from Thomas Wentworth Higginson, to Fannie Eckstorm, was included in the Appendix. The letter was in regards to Eckstorm's analysis on Thoreau's *The Maine Woods*. Here that letter is reproduced in entirety as a preface to Higginson's essay on his climb of Katahdin. His essay titled, *Going to Mount Katahdin,* appeared in the September 1856 issue of *Putnam's Monthly* magazine. The account is of interest because of Higginson's acknowledgment to Eckstorm that while the article appears to have been written from a woman's perspective, it was Higginson himself who penned the article. The essay was reprinted in Volume XVIII of *Appalachia* (Publisher, Appalachian Mountain Club) in June 1925 with an explanation that Higginson, who in 1885 had been President of the Appalachian Mountain Club, had indeed written the article.

The Higginson essay documents the third known trip where a group of women had ascended the mountain. Assuredly, the accuracy of who climbed such a remote mountain, at specific dates in those early years, can never be assessed with certainty. However, based on the published newspaper articles, the Higginson expedition appears as the third ascent by women. This is of historical interest in that it was organized by Higginson, who, aside from being a colonel, minister, poet, editor, and writer, was an early supporter of women's rights, and an advocate for a more casual dress code for the female sex. This interest is contained in the descriptions of this trip, where Higginson adds the details of the outfits the ladies acquired once in the backwoods of Maine.

Within the article, the anonymous writer, makes mention of the following:

"Friends," said I, "we have been basely deceived. H., who was to have been historiographer of our feminine expedition, has fled to foreign parts, and is probably at this moment standing on the Pico d'Azores,[18] which is two thousand feet higher than even Katahdin. Nevertheless, that history is to be written, if I write it myself."

This paragraph, while alluding to Higginson as "missing," in reality provides the truth of the author's location. Over the winter of 1855/1856 Higginson, and his first wife, Mary Channing, who was in ill health, spent six months in the Azores. While in the region at that time, Higginson wrote of his climb to the summit of Mount Pico in April of 1856.[19]

---

[18] Referring to Ponta do Pico, which is the highest mountain in the Azores at 7,713 feet. It could be he penned the Katahdin article for Putnam's Monthly while in the Azores.

[19] Thomas Wentworth Higginson, "The Ascent of Pico," Manuscript Journals, in the Houghton Library, Harvard University, Cambridge, MA.

Prior to the 1855 Higginson expedition, there are two documented prior hiking groups with a focus on women being included. In August of 1849, a party with two women climbers left a note in a bottle at the Pamola peak around the 11th of that month. The women have been identified as Mrs. Elizabeth Oakes Smith, of Brooklyn, New York (but originally from Maine), and Mrs. Nancy Crockett Mosman, of Bangor, Maine. The second group, consisting of five women, had climbed the mountain on August 20th of that same year, and had discovered the bottle left by the first group.

The account of the third group of women climbers of Katahdin is given in the included essay. The names of the climbers have recently been pieced together through literature detective work. [20] The readers of the following story may be interested in the real names, and the pseudonyms, Higginson used in the essay for the women. These are as compiled by William Geller in the noted reference.

Lucy Chase, Pilgrim, Alice.
Sarah Chase, Quaker opera dancer, Fanny or Kate.
Martha Gordon, Stage struck nun, Fanny or Kate.
Mary LeBaron, Little Bo-peep, Mary.
Rebekah Northey, La Fille duRegiment, Rachel.

---

[20] For a full account of the first three documented ascents of Mount Katahdin by women, see, "The Mount Katahdin Peaks: the First 12 Women Climbers, 1849-1855," by William W. Geller. The article is available from DigitalCommons from a search on the internet.

These ladies were accompanied by:

Amory Battles, Bangor, ME. (Due to a family emergency, he only traveled from Bangor to Orono with the party.)

Albert Brown, Worcester, Massachusetts.

Theophilus (Theo) Brown, Worcester, Massachusetts.

Mr. Chase, Waterville, ME.

Thomas Higginson, Worcester, Massachusetts.

> *With the loss of Amory Battles, this gives four men who made the climb of Katahdin, not including the guides, as part of the party. Yet, by all counts there were five. The essay also includes the name "Alfred," who is not identified even in the Geller paper, as the fifth man.*

Ben Mosher, teamster & guide.

Alex McClane and John E. Stacey – the guides.

While now we know the essay was penned by Higginson, we do not know why he decided to keep the names a secret at the time and to never have divulged them in full. It was common in the era that stories were submitted to magazines with initials, partial names, or pseudonyms, and he may have been simply keeping with convention. A key theme in his article is that the trip was made with the five women and an important mention was their attire for hiking in the Maine woods and throwing convention of the day to the wind.

The following 1908 letter from Higginson to Eckstorm, was in the collection of Donald H. Williams and was mentioned in a 1965 article that appeared in the *Colby Library*

Quarterly.[21] Williams was a correspondent with Eckstorm for several years prior to her death. The two shared an interest in Maine literature and Eckstorm sent Williams many original Maine books she held in her collection.

Higginson addresses Eckstorm as, Miss, as maybe he did not know she was married. The original published article, to which Higginson is referring, published Eckstorm's first name incorrectly as Fanny. A full analysis of her Thoreau article Higginson refers to, is covered in the book, *Exploring the Maine Woods – The Hardy Family Expedition to the Machias Lakes.*

Ipswich, Mass.
Aug 10, 1908

Dear Miss Eckstorm

Allow one of the very oldest of contributors (still living) for the Atlantic Monthly to thank you heartily for the best paper in the August number - your review of his "Maine Woods". I knew Thoreau well and was one of the most devoted readers of his "Concord & Merrimac Rivers", but have never seen his limitations so skillfully analyzed. Moreover, I take especial interest in your Katahdin stories, having been there myself once a humble explorer there, at an early period, having published a paper called, *Going to*

---

[21] Williams, H. Donald, "T. W. Higginson on Thoreau and Maine." Colby Library Quarterly, ser. 7, no. 1, March 1965, p. 29-32.

Mt. Katahdin, in the (original) Putnam's Magazine for September, 1856. Even if you have happened to see the article you may never have learned that it was written by a man & not a woman, being sent out by me to puzzle the five ladies who were engaged with me in that delightfully pioneer enterprise. Three of these companions have since died, but two of them (Misses Lucy and Sarah Chase) are still living in Worcester Mass as is one of the male members, Mr. Brown also in Worcester. It may interest you to know that Thoreau's most intimate friend & outdoor companion, Rev. H. G. O. Blake of Worcester was to have been of the party & was actually on his way, by my side, in the railway car, when he coughed up a slight discharge of blood & informed me that he must go back, which he did.

I have also written a story with the scene laid on the way to Mt. Ktaadn, but of little value.

Very cordially yours
Thomas
Wentworth
Higginson
(aet. 84)

The following are the characters noted in the story with their aliases and real names, as best can be determined:

- (I) or H, the narrator, the historiographer, Thomas W. Higginson.

- L, H's friend from Bangor, Amory Battles – did not attend the entire trip because in Orono he received a telegram that, Annie (a family member), had taken ill.

- Mr. C, L's replacement, Mr. Chase.

- Mr. B., Albert Brown.

- Theo, Theophilus Brown.
- Alfred, no further information discovered.
- Fanny or Kate, Quaker opera dancer, Sarah Chase.
- Fanny or Kate, Stage struck nun, Martha Gordon.
  *not separately identified.
- Alice, or Pilgrim, Lucy Chase.
- Mary, Little Bo-peep, Mary LeBaron.
- Rachel, La Fille duRegiment, Rebekah Northey.
- Ben Mosher – teamster & guide.
- Alick (Alex) McClane – Guide.
- John E. Stacey – Guide.
- Mr. Wildfire, unknown man met on the trail.
- Mirch, hired hand.

PUTNAM'S MONTHLY.

A Magazine of Literature, Science, and Art.

VOL. VIII.—SEPTEMBER, 1856.—NO. XLV.

GOING TO MOUNT KATAHDIN[22]

No name was given on the original published article.

LAST night I dreamed of Katahdin. Masculine tyranny had kept me, as a woman, in the house all day, on pretense of storms, which looked really worse from inside than outside. It

---

[22] Original text, except the new footnotes which are copyright to this book to add clarification where necessary.

was a wild, cold night, and the little comfortable fire, that smouldered on the hearth, was dying away as I went to sleep. The rail-roads were choked with snow; but in five minutes I had traveled the three hundred miles, and was in those happy woods again. It was September once more, and we were in our camp by the lake. Breezes from the monarch of eastern mountains stirred the tall tree-tops above our heads; the soft plash of the water came faintly through the white birch trees; and was it a moose's slender feet upon the twigs, or some crackling artillery among the green bushes on the fire? I felt the softness of the hemlock couch beneath me — freshest and most fragrant of beds,[23] where I never sought sleep in vain. Half awake, I raised myself, leaning against the tent stakes, as I had done so often. There was the little cleared circle amid the woods, lighted and limited by the smouldering fire. One great log, that hissed with a soothing sound of slow burning, sent sometimes a shower of sparks into the night air, and sometimes dropped its tribute of brilliants into the pit of intenser light beneath it. The embers before the tent of our masculine companions were low and dim, and, from the woods beyond, came the smothered stroke of an axe, wielded by the strong arm of guide or friends, risen at midnight to replenish them. But our domestic flames flickered on the scattered traces of our daily employments: pots, kettles, and birch-bark platters; three partridges hanging upon one branch, a string of fish upon another; a pile of tin dippers against a mossy root; Fanny's shoes drying on the ashes, and Rachel's

---

[23] Take note here of Higginson's mention of hemlock for bedding. The preference for hemlock will again be mentioned in a letter from Manly Hardy in a later chapter.

immaculate little white sun-bonnet on a projecting branch of
the tent-pole. Above, the stars burned in keen eagerness
through the black sky; around, the circle of trees stood,
illuminated sentinels; black, flickering shadows were blotted
in behind them; and behind these lay the interminable forests
of Maine.

Suddenly the wind seemed to blow more wildly. What
woodland bird or beast was it, pray, that gave that strange
sound, like a combination of shivered window-glass and a
crashing blind? Instantly the light vanished, as I started up,
broad awake, exclaiming: "Girls! Kate, Fanny, the campfire is
out!" when a blast such as I never felt in the forest blew
through the broken pane; and I knew that it was January, not
September—and a chamber, not a camp. The next day I went
to Fanny's house. Fanny was at home.

"Friends," said I, "we have been basely deceived. H., who
was to have been historiographer of our feminine expedition,
has fled to foreign parts, and is probably at this moment
standing on the Pico d'Azores, which is two thousand feet
higher than even Katahdin. Nevertheless, that history is to be
written, if I write it myself." So here it follows:

For more than a year, we had clearly resolved to go to the
top of Katahdin, which, as everybody knows, is deep in the
forests of Maine, and is the highest ground in New England,
except Mount Washington. During the whole summer, L., at
Bangor, and H., at home, had corresponded with the
voluminous which gentlemen always think necessary when
anything entertaining is to be done. H., also, in well-meant but
rather superfluous precaution, was constantly calling at our
houses during the last month, on various pretexts, but always
happening to close with the inquiry whether our Bloomer

dresses were ready for the woods, and an additional hint as to the importance of wearing our new calf-skin boots a good deal before hand, so as to accustom the feet to pedestrian labors, etc., etc. Of course, we needed no such suggestions. Accordingly, the boots of two out of the five were sent home precisely twelve hours before departing; and the last stitches were put to the wardrobe of at least one, at a much later period. My impression is, that that stitch in time did not save nine subsequently. What could the staid conductor on the Eastern Railroad have thought of our state of spirits that night? What the dignified statesman thought — our opposite neighbor in the car — was painted in his countenance. But if he had been a signer of the Declaration of Independence, it would not have sobered us. We had signed one ourselves. Anxious mothers and doubting papas were behind us (it might be for weeks, but we knew it could not be forever), and we had before us the radiant days of early September, and a fortnight of freedom in the woods. Ingenuity itself could not discover anything to be anxious about. So many little things might have interfered, and none did. There was not even a cold among us, and nobody had forgotten her carpet-bag.

On board the steamer from Portland to Bangor we began to live according to nature; that is, we went to bed with the moon, and rose with the sun. It was lovely, up the Penobscot, passing somewhere that singular, stony mountain of which Theo, declared, that if it were struck by lightning, the lightning would get the worst of it. At last appeared the wharf; there was Bangor, but there was not L. We needed a check to our triumph, and we had one. We went to the Bangor House, and felt for a moment a little blank, as L. alone was to make our arrangements. However, we packed our cares on H.'s shoulders, and sent him off to explore, while Alice and I took our own way to dispel our griefs, by going shopping for shoes, veils, and gloves, additional, at the last moment.

Presently, L. and sunshine came into the room together; they always hunt in couples. After him came Ben, our future driver, philosopher, and friend, six feet and a fraction; Yankee to the backbone, and plenty of *that*; slim, straight, and keen-eyed, with long black locks, and also two ends of blue ribbon, four times longer, depending from his hat; probably a triumphal decoration for the ladies' trip to Katahdin. I remember nothing more till we found ourselves behind Ben's three horses, at four and a half P. M., on the road from Bangor to Orono, riding among river views which I believe are good in reality, and which certainly are quite celestial in my memory. Ten precious souls, with their bodies; and dear sturdy L. had plenty of both. Projector, patron, and purveyor of our expedition, he never looked so happy when preaching his best sermon, or bringing home his largest moose, as when he had thus his adopted children fairly within his reach, on their way to the wonders he had promised them. How little he expected our first pause would bring him (at Orono) the telegraphic news of dear little Annie's sickness, and that he must leave us, with a heavy heart, at the very entrance of our promised land.

How we ever got over his departure, we never clearly understood. It shows what a state of spirits we were in. Indeed, at first, it hung upon a breath whether we should go on, or turn back. Happily the breath was L.'s, and we went on. But fancy a pleasure-party in a boat, with only one sailor among them, and he stepping on shore as they leave the wharf. Yet who had ever dreamed of a boat as longingly as we had dreamed of Katahdin? When I say we went on without L., therefore, I say something wonderful. Happily, we took in Mr. C., himself a sturdy prop, and especially charged by L., with our support. Mr. B. had joined us at Bangor, so we were still ten precious souls, though we felt a trifle less precious than before.

How that cool, rich evening air wiped out our sorrows! Yes, a little damp, if you insist upon it. But there we were, in an open wagon, on a cloudless night, and we were on the way to Katahdin; and there was the low and winding Penobscot, and the early stars above its meadows; and these cottages were Maine farm-houses, and so all was delightful; and we talked, and laughed, and made acquaintance with our new recruits, and sang the songs for the first time, which we were never to hear the last of. And we rode through Old Town, with its mills and looms; and Sunkhaze,[24] where we could not find that anything was ever sunk, except a horse and his rider in the mud, about whom the usual story is told. And there is a still better story, viz., that a certain spirit, conversing through his medium in Bangor, and declaring his position to be in the unmentionable region of perpetual warmth, stated (on being asked for minuter details), that the said place was far, far worse than Old Town, and almost as bad as Sunkhaze.

We spent that night at Greenbush, twenty-two miles from Bangor. It was a good beginning. Theo. was confident that he had heard the cry of a wolf,[25] and we had everything

---

[24] Sunkhaze Meadows, a peat bog, is on the east bank of the Penobscot, north of Old Town, is now home to a wildlife refuge.
[25] Possibly so, since wolves were not extirpated from Maine until the 1890s. Single wolf killings in Maine were reported in 1993 and 1996; the origin of the animals was unknown. A hybrid of coyote and the western wolf are said to exist in Maine.

comfortable about us. In the evening we called in experts to testify as to routes and guides. These gentlemen tipped back their chairs and gave familiar lectures with great gusto; slashing into our prejudices without mercy, objecting to our favorite plan of approach (though we took it after all), and setting down our expected guide with "Law! he's an old hen!" (N. B.[26] We didn't take him, but he isn't!)

In the morning, some of us were amused by the comments of our advisers and others on our expedition. "Don't yer suppose, now, them gals will have a better time than if they'd gone to Saratogue or them places?" "Think likely!" ejaculated another. "Git to the top of Katahdin, will they, think?" "Law, no!" was the reply; "but they think they're goin' to, and they'll have just as good fun as if they did!"

The gentlemen began to shed civilization at Greenbush, and showed a tendency to brilliant shirts, while we postponed our October hues for two days longer. But the change gave us a little the air of a circus company as we rode along, and contributed to the excitement of the Penobscot valley. Our wagon had three seats, holding three each, besides room for three more passengers, viz., two on the great iron guards to the wheels, and one on the barrel of hard bread that was made fast behind. These places being extremely uncomfortable, were of course the favorites with the gentlemen of the party. These scarlet outriders gave breadth as well as color to the equipage;

---

[26] N.B. is an abbreviation for "note well." Sometimes this was written as, NB or n.b., and is meant to draw the reader's attention to an aside. As for this note, the writer may have been referring to either Brad Webber or Bill Chesley who are noted on the following page.

and it was quite impressive to walk on before the wagon and look back, as our three stout horses toiled up long hills in Ben's energetic hands, or Kate's, sometimes.

It was a great moment when we first came in sight of Katahdin; in fact it called forth the first of those triplets of rather shrill hurras which afterwards marked all important eras of our expedition, and some unimportant ones. There stood the great, bare, lonely, steep, blue magnificence, as marked in outline as Monadnock,[27] but more absolutely isolated, more precipitous, more sublime; its square top, not yet broken by nearness into volcano-like jags, but the whiteness of its many broad slides gleaming afar off, and rather fearfully.

All day we kept his majesty in sight, and he seemed to withdraw or bring near his august form, as the vapors gathered or dissolved around him—delicate vapors, never a cloud.

We were surprised all along here, first at the openness of the country, and then at the size of the villages; indeed, we afterwards heard expressions of astonishment that we had been willing to go through the cities in such costume. The cities were Lincoln and Mettawamkeag. There anxieties about guides began. We could find neither "Brad Webber," nor "Bill Chesley," but were happy in securing the aid of "Alick McClane," a vigorous specimen of resolute manhood, who looked as if he could go anywhere, and accomplish anything, unless turning back made a part of the duty. His measure was

---

[27] Mt. Monadnock, or Grand Monadnock, is a 3,165 ft. mountain in the towns of Jaffrey and Dublin, New Hampshire. It would have been well-known to these explorers who lived not far south, in and near to Worcester, Massachusetts.

easily given to us, in the lumberer's scale — "Can charge his six dollars a day, in spring, as 'head of a drive,' and get it, too."

Our horses were tired, but we were bound to reach "Hunt's,"[28] the last house on our route, by the morrow night. So we must push on seven miles further, after dark, walking much of the way. The road changed, and led through deep woods. How wild it was, to press on before the rest, with a single companion, lighted by stars, glow worms, and a lantern; no house, endless woods full of possible bears, and no sound but the lumbering of the wagon behind, and an occasional burst of song. Yet welcome at last, near midnight, was the light of the South Moluncas Hotel,[29] at the foot of the Aroostook road.

We had already heard of a dance, this night, at this very hotel, and that was one of our reasons for resolving to get there, though Ben, our driver, had promised us a sleepless night in consequence. To be sure, he admitted, these balls were nothing to the times in spring, when the lumbermen came out of the woods, to these rural inns.

"Lively doings then?" asked we.

"I tell you," quoth Ben, energetically, "the things they don't say and do, ain't worth thinking of!"

---

[28] Hunt's Farm was started around 1835 by William Hunt as a supply depot for logging operations.

[29] Thoreau visited this public house in 1846. He wrote, "we rode on up the Houlton Road seven miles, to Molunkus, ..., where there is a spacious public house in the woods, called "Molunkus House," ..., which looked as if it had its hall for dancing and military drills." (In, *"Ktaadn – The Maine Woods."*)

After this preparation, we were astonished at the quietness of the establishment; but the ball had turned out rather a failure, and the youths and maidens were as well dressed and as tame as in Boston. They were just going to supper, and we were too tired to sit up for the renewal of festivities; but Ben did, and said he told them that our party would have made their dance "enough sight livelier." He had already learned to appreciate us, that was evident.

We waked fresh and bright, and so did the morning; in the little parlor we found a spirited damsel who had been in the second party of women to the mountains (Mrs. E. O. Smith's being the first, and ours the third).[30] Her account was slightly fearful; they spent eight days in the woods, and when they got back from "Hunt's," she had to be lifted out of the wagon. We looked at ours, and inwardly vowed we would not sink to that degradation, even if we had to roll over the bread-barrel in the rear. But we now knew what was before us — twenty-five miles of forest walking, each way, not more than we expected; but first we must get to the terminus — "Hunt's."

To relieve Ben's horses, four of us got into a stage wagon that passed, and rode eighteen miles to our dining-place,

---

[30] The first two women, in documented accounts, are reported to have been Elizabeth Oakes Smith and Nancy Crockett Mosman in August of 1849. The second group of five women, also of that month and year were Carline T. Eastman, Martha L. Mason, Esther Jones, Almira Lowder, and Hannah Taylor. Higginson does not give a name for the woman they met at the Moluncas Hotel. For an excellent account see, Geller, William W., "*The Mount Katahdin Peaks: The First 12 Women Climbers, 1849-1855,*" (2016). Maine History Documents. Available online from DigitalCommons@UMaine.

"Number Three." Our fame had traveled before us, and the driver eagerly asked which of the ladies was Lucy Stone?[31] We thought of assuming her laurels, as there was no great danger of being called on for a speech, and we could safely crow when going into the woods; but we told the truth at last, that she was not of our party. It seemed that there had been in Bangor a rumor of her coming with us. That was surely a delicious ride, along the Aroostook road; genuine Maine, at length; woods not very ancient, indeed, but unbroken; up sudden hills, and down into perilous valleys where the wheels were braked; on, on, among bright leaves and tall dead stems draperied with lichens and mosses; scarcely a clearing in the distance, but constant glimpses of the great lonely Katahdin, pale blue against the sky, square and stern, his sides scarred whiter than ever, and opening his vast crater more and more upon a nearer and profile view.

We had got beyond towns with names to them. Township, No. 1 (in the fifth range), has four families. No. 2 is, or was, owned by the Roman Catholic bishop of Boston, and is settled by Irish wholly. It is sometimes called Benedicta. No. 3 is a very little settlement; yet the tavern at which we dined had been occupied sixteen years; it is supported wholly by the lumber business, and a kind old lady looked up from her knitting to inform us that eighteen or twenty *horses* stopped there every night, and in winter, thirty or forty. The human statistics seemed less important.

---

[31] Lucy Stone (1818 – 1893) of West Brookfield, Massachusetts was an abolitionist and a vocal advocate and organizer promoting rights for women. There seems to have been a mistaking of the parties own Lucy Chase for Lucy Stone.

At this place, as everywhere else, our party called forth much wonder, more compliments than wonder, and more good advice than compliments. On this occasion, we were warned, among other things, not to expect to get to Hunt's that night. It was hard to bear this, as much of our plans depended on that point. It was only ten miles, by the road, if it only had been a road. But the ride turned out a walk, for most of us, and the first five miles took nearly three hours. And the lumber road made Pinkham Notch look smooth, and the North Conway paths appear English lawns. Yet, how lovely it was to walk through those endless woods into the dying day, the long rank under-growth filling up the intervals of the trees, and, at every step, some splendor amid the greenery, or dark blue dracoena berries, or the gorgeous scarlet seeds of the arum. Lovely, until some sudden plunge of a gentleman into a bog (for the ladies were more carefully guided), or of a wagon wheel into some gap in the "corduroy road," brought the procession to a precipitate halt, amid unfailing and joyous laughter. Thus early were the strength and spirits of the party tested— a thing most important; for it is precisely the same mishaps and misadventures which bring dismay to the timid traveler, and make up half the enjoyment of the journey to the sunny and strong.

The sun was low when we reached, not Hunt's farm-house, but Stacy's, the only previous one, and half the distance. Here we held a council, abandoned at once our cherished hope, and in ten minutes had formed our usual line from wagon to entry, passed in shawls, cloaks, valises (one apiece), and all smaller commodities, while Ben had unharnessed his horses, and McClane and Mr. C. started on foot for Hunt's, to make arrangements for the morrow. The little house swelled to receive us; two prompt and lady-like maidens moved quietly about to make preparations; a delightful farmer's supper was soon ready, (and such appetites!) and we settled down for the night, pleased and surprised at our most unexpected quarters.

This detention was the one great success of our journey. We stopped for a night's lodging, and found a treasure. The fact was, we still had felt rather anxious about our guides. McClane was admirable; but we needed two; besides, he had never ascended the mountain on this side, and we knew the inconvenience which the slightest mistake in our course might produce. Our one desideratum was, a guide in whose knowledge of the route we might feel implicit confidence, and we found him here. John Stacy — the fine-looking youth in a red shirt, who went in and out occasionally as we sat at table — not only turned out to be (as we afterwards discovered) the best woodsman in that region, but had actually been one of the party which spotted, as it is termed, the only path through the woods to Katahdin, on this side. No wonder we eagerly clutched at such a prize; but we evidently had a reciprocal attraction, for though he had to leave his grain unshorn (as in the Scotch ballad), he, at last, forsook it and followed. Yes, we had reason to be grateful for our delay at that pleasant farmhouse, with the original log-cabin beside it, in which this really refined and agreeable family had been born and bred; and, with the noble view of Katahdin close by, which, tired as we were, we must go out and see before light failed us. Nay, the house seemed a half-way house to Katahdin; for the memory of Mrs. E. O. Smith's visit was still a fruitful subject of conversation; and we found, on referring to the journal of a certain friend (which we had brought with us), that he also had stopped here, ten years before, and had praised the same household attributes which we admired.

We slept that night in large rooms, unfinished, so that our neighbors' lights glimmered through the laths, and every voice in the house sounded close to our ears. It was easy to wake each other up next day; indeed, peals of laughter did that unconsciously. For a great transformation took place that morning; and we, who left the parlor at night, robed in the bedrabbled skirts of civilization, reappeared at breakfast, metamorphosed into free and happy "Bloomers."[32]

Be it known, that we had always been special opponents of the "short dress," as it is more mildly termed by its friends, and had delayed assuming it as long as possible. But yesterday's mud had settled that question, so down we came, in our very melo-dramatic costume. The gentlemen tried to spare our feelings; but it must be confessed, that our feet trod uneasily in the unaccustomed daylight.

Shall I describe the dresses? First, Fanny and Kate came shyly in, attired alike in slate-colored suits, trimmed with an almost invisible blue cord; there was, also, a glimpse of not quite invisible blue stockings, just above the substantial shoes—the sombreness of their dresses being relieved by little jaunty felt hats and colored ribbons. They were declared to

---

[32] A common name for the articles of clothing for women during the reforms of the 1800s toward more casual attire. The term, bloomers, is associated with Amelia Jenks Bloomer (1818 – 1894), an American women's rights advocate. Bloomer published *The Lily* newspaper in which she included her defense of the *short more-casual outfit* and led to the dress being called Bloomers. Other names were the American Dress, or reform dress.

resemble stage-struck nuns, or Quaker opera-dancers. Next, Alice tried to escape observation, by hiding her face beneath a broad straw hat; but her scarlet trimmings, on a plain dark skirt and jacket, made her both conspicuous and picturesque. The two remaining damsels put on a bold face, laughed at themselves, and stood up to be looked at. Mistress Mary wore a chocolate-colored suit, corded with scarlet, and a white felt hat; a pair of boots hung at her belt (the only genuine pair in the party), and she carried a long staff, like little Bo-peep in the picture. Finally, came Rachel, whose costume was at once admitted, without envy, to be the crowning triumph. Her dress was blue and drab, with broad blue trimmings, and the trowsers gathered in at the ankle, were very becoming to the little booted feet. She wore a white sun-bonnet (which staid white to the last), lined with blue; and the tin cup at her belt completed her resemblance to La Fille du Regiment,[33] with her canteen.

The five gentlemen's costumes I must be excused from describing; they looked sturdy and comfortable in various combinations of blue and red shirts and frocks, with black belts for knives and cups. In some cases they even looked picturesque, especially Theo. in a red fancy shirt, borrowed from some friendly fireman, and decorated with large white stars and white spread-eagles, upside down. Beside these, we

---

[33] La Fille du Régiment (*The Daughter of the Regiment*) was an 1840 French opéra comique. The character, Marie, was the vivandière (canteen girl) of the Regiment. Here 'daughter' could be taken as mascot. The vivandiere were women who attached themselves to the army in a sanctioned role to sell wine and provisions to the soldiers. In many cases, wives of soldiers traveled with the army in this role.

had our two guides and our trusty driver, Ben; all three having served their time in a lumber-camp, and knowing on which side of a pine tree to look for the north.

A few hours of the morning brought us to that desire of our hearts, Hunt's farm-house; and it proved as delightful a spot as we had fancied. It is the end of inhabited Maine in this direction, and an important place to the lumberers in the logging season. Here is a little green clearing on the high bank of the lovely "East Branch" (Penobscot), which here makes a bend round a point of forest; wooded mountains rise behind, hiding King Katahdin. The farm-house was defined by Theo. as being "very small outside, and very large inside—the proper way to build a house;" it is of logs, squared and boarded over, and it contains the most stupendous of kitchen fireplaces, and the cheeriest of hostesses. Their last previous visitor was Church,[34] the artist, who had just been spending some time there. None of us had ever seen him, but we wished that he had staid long enough to accompany and illustrate our march; and we wished, also, for jovial John P. Hale,[35] whom we heard of down below, at South Moluncas, idling away his time in making stump speeches, instead of going beyond the stumps into the forest with us.

---

[34] Frederic Church, the artist. For additional background on Church and his life in these woods, see, *Thomas S. Steele's Maine Adventures*, the two-book compilation of *Canoe and Camera* and *Paddle and Portage*, from Tommy Carbone (Burnt Jacket Publishing).

[35] John Parker Hale (1806 – 1873) an American politician and lawyer from New Hampshire.

Meanwhile, the gentlemen proceeded to "make up their packs" in the most scientific manner, on the grass before the house. Packs are made thus: a square blanket or coarse shawl is spread on the ground, and the contents placed on one corner; then rolled over and over, till the other corner is reached, which is securely pinned with a wooden peg. The two ends of this long roll are then brought together and also pinned; and the whole slung over the victim's shoulders. We had reduced our baggage to a minimum, or minimissimum, for six days. But add nearly a barrelful of hard bread, fifteen pounds of sugar, thirty pounds of pork, twenty pounds of tea, beside two tents, cooking utensils, gun, axe, and sundries, and you will perceive that the sinews of our masculine friends were likely to be pretty well tested.

After a good dinner, we left Hunt's, with three cheers. Crossing the river in a bateau, we struck at once into a forest-path, that led—to Katahdin! Fifty miles of forest and mountain were before us, including the return walk; but we had a cloudless sky, happy hearts, trustworthy companions, and comfortable shoes. Thanks to the practice of the two preceding days, we were somewhat inured to walking; and to this, and our moderate speed at the outset, was attributed our entire freedom from blistered feet, the most common discomfort of pedestrians. Mr. Hunt was to go with us a few miles, to convey our load as far as possible, in his little two-horse cart, or "jumper;" but the jumper soon jumped once too often, over a stone, and broke down, and the packs had to be shouldered.

The fresh delight of that first after noon's walk, with the world behind us, and the woods before, can neither be described nor forgotten. It was too delicious to be real, and too genuine to be ideal. We walked along a grassy path, cut to carry provisions to the lumber camps in winter, as we saw by a few scattered traces — here a sled among the bushes, there a vast empty cask. These were all but concealed by the luxuriant undergrowth. We walked among great golden rods, and coarse white asters, higher than our heads, and were never far from the shallow, rippling river. Here and there some tree had fallen across the road, or some rude bridge been swept away from a water-course: if there had been no difficulties to surmount, we should not have known the luxury of our new costume. We heard with special satisfaction the first woodman's rule, that H. imparted: "never step on anything which you can step over;" for he little knew what a novelty it was to us, to be able to step over anything.

We could scarcely believe that we had walked six leisurely miles, when we reached our first camping-ground, at sunset. "Already!" was the universal cry, as, two by two, we came down with delighted surprise into the little forest dingle, where the blue smoke already curled up through the stately trees, and we could see McClane spreading tents, while Stacy unrolled packs, and old Mirch (an assistant brought with us from Hunt's, for this day only) busied himself among his scanty kettles and pans. We women-folk were soon a picturesque group of semi-fatigue, beneath the trees; but presently hastened to join in the feminine avocation of bed making. In this case, the bedstead was a spot of earth, from which all stubs and stumps had been smoothed away by the axe; and the bed consisted of three or four layers of ends of hemlock boughs, laid regularly, in shingle fashion, over the whole surface. This being thoroughly done, and a thickness or two of blanket laid over it, the result is luxury. Pillows we had none, or only the ancient Egyptian style, namely, a log of wood.

After a while, Fanny, Rachel, and I, wandered off to the riverside, first crossing a brook, by a fallen tree, in the fading light. We had left the East Branch behind us, and sat now watching the pretty whirling ripples of the wild Wissatacook,[36] swiftest of the Penobscot's tributaries. At last, then, we had entered on our gipsy life. Would all be happy as now, or would rains and disasters follow! Would the joyous thoughts and refreshing existence of the woods only come and go away useless, like those water-drops down the river, or lead our aspirations, like the blue smoke, upward? Suddenly the smoke suggested other thoughts, and we went back to the camp, and for the first time in our lives, tasted fried pork and crackers. Well, it was not quite unsuccessful, and we hoped for something better tomorrow, and had it. Tea without milk was not intolerable either, only so great were the demands upon the sugar, that Mr. B. became its guardian, at once, and kept close the string of the sack. We sat up awhile; for it did not take long to "clear away the things;" we looked at the stars, and the fire, and the trees, and each other, and the picturesque red-shirted figures passing to and fro with great logs, or with water pails; we were very happy; we sung songs and hymns; and did not like it overmuch, when H., beginning thus promptly his tyranny, sent us to bed very early, and then sat up himself. How inconceivably strange it was, to lie on the ground, wrapped in our blankets, with only a tent above our heads, and a campfire before us; for the tent, of course, was open on that side. The air seemed cool, if we popped our heads out into it;

---

[36] Wassataquoik on current maps, and as labeled on Hubbard's 1899 map. See, *Hubbard's Guide to Moosehead Lake and Northern Maine, Annotated Edition*, (2020).

but the tent was full of warmth — sometimes too much warmth — and occasionally, though rarely, a trifle of smoke. For me, I lay awake an hour, and then slept, I may say, enthusiastically. One or two were less fortunate; but they declared it was worth lying awake for. No sound but the wind in the trees, and the crackling flames—think of it!

Besides early bed-time, H. established a rule that we should rise every day at five, and the ladies should have exclusive possession of the forest and river for half an hour, the gentlemen taking their turn afterwards.

To these delightful morning ablutions, we owed, no doubt, much of the health and comfort of the journey. At six we breakfasted — fried pork and crackers for the second and last time. We had brought no other provisions (except tea and sugar), relying on the woods to furnish our supplies, which, so far, they had not done. Still, we were glad to have to come down to the simplest fare at the outset, so as to know that we could do it. Indeed, in respect to fried pork and crackers, one finds after a day's tramp, that — but perhaps I had better stop.

At any rate, the gentlemen were pleased to compliment our freshness of appearance in the morning, nor was Stacy, our guide, content with this partial encomium. (I intend to write the whole truth, the whole, or none.) Said H., who had observed his scrutinizing eye dwelling on one or another of the party, "Mr. Stacy, will these ladies get through to the top!"

"That's what they *will* do," responded he, energetically. "I tell you, there's no better grit to be scared up anywhere than those women have!" If we had quailed for one moment during the excursion, these words would have inspired us again.

While the final preparations were being made, we watched with a sort of lingering regret the smouldering remains of our fire, dying away into blank daylight. At seven we left, with packs somewhat diminished in weight, the gentlemen remarked at first. I believe that after a mile or two they changed their opinion. Our way at first led along a high bank, above the river, through the same rank growth of aster and goldenrod; we went strolling on, with our long staves of black birch, beneath trees higher than before; still no scrambling or real difficulty yet. Sometimes we stopped to rest; once at a deserted lumberers' camp, built of logs, with fireplace in the middle, "deacon seat" on each side, and sleeping-places still littered with decayed fir-boughs, behind. Close by, stood the stable — a more imposing edifice than the house. During these halts, Alfred would make impetuous efforts to catch fish, while Ben strolled before us with a gun, having about equal success, that is, none at all

At last we must leave our friendly path, ford the river, and plunge into deeper woods. The transit was effected by aid of our strong guides, who grasped hands, and thus gave us a seat between them. H., however, having had some experience in carrying invalid ladies, was moved to transport Alice alone. The water was not more than knee deep, but very rapid, and the bottom consisted of large, round, slippery stones; we were, therefore, not surprised, before he reached the opposite shore, to see him sink suddenly on one knee, where he quietly remained, afraid to attempt to recover himself, and holding Alice aloft, until help came in the shape of Stacy. She escaped with only a wet foot, but we all had that soon; for we presently plunged into the most inexplicable bog which we anywhere encountered. Evidently some mountain stream had hurried through there in the spring, carrying a lapful of logs to play with, and had never taken the trouble to clear them away afterwards; so we played puss-in-the-corner with them ourselves, up and down, now in, now out — jumping from clump to clump of grass, amid black mud, in which our boots sank full fathoms five, and our feet became mere cork-screws to pull them out again; then chancing on little dells of lovely Linnaea,[37] still in bloom, and stopping to decorate our hats with its long sprays of soft leaves and nodding flowers, soon to be torn off, perhaps, by overhanging boughs. The great white berries of the delicate creeping snowberry were also beneath our feet, and we refreshed ourselves with these; Stacy first pronouncing them innocent. We saw also berries of trillium, Solomon's seal, dwarf cornel, and dracaena.

Then we took our course upward, having to skirt a smaller eminence before coming in sight of Katahdin. There was only the vestige of a path, which we soon became expert in tracing; as also in detecting the "spots" on trees, where previous explorers had struck off a chip with an axe, for guidance. Sometimes, however, even Stacy was in doubt, and we halted willingly till his cheery voice rang through the woods. Often, too, we halted with no such good reason. For we varied in speed, of course, and it was very pleasant, at some place where a clear spring oozed from the rich black earth, to halt and drink from our tin cups, and look back on red and blue figures winding through the woods, while each of our brethren, as he came up, unslung the weary pack from his shoulders, and some companion damsel, perhaps, seated herself at once upon it, or lay reclined upon the moss, gazing up at the heaven between the tree-tops. No wild beasts, nor wild men, only a partridge

---

[37] Linnaea, a plant genus in the family Caprifoliaceae, the honeysuckle family.

whirred away when the gun was in the wrong place. To be sure, an advance party once saw a bear, but he quickly retreated; however, we all saw bear tracks, and fresh deer tracks everywhere. As for men, we found the names of two youths of our acquaintance recorded on a tree, where we crossed the Wissaticook,[38] and we appended our own beneath them. We elsewhere found one of their night-camps, skillfully built of boughs and hemlock bark. There were few flowers, and the trees were not so large as we had expected; though sometimes a magnificent pine towered amid the second growth, memorial of a time when maidens, duskier and more agile than we, chanted their murmuring songs beneath its boughs.

At such times, also, we could compare notes of experience, and have leisure for Theo.'s jokes, and the woodland lore of the guides. It was wonderful how many different themes the pine woods led to. It is said that western roads often dwindle to a squirrel track, and run up a tree, but our talk ran up the trees first, and then far away. Who would think, for instance, of any connection between Katahdin and the Crimea?[39] But we learned that the war had raised the value of bearskins, in these forests, to fourteen dollars. Then we broached the Darien expedition,[40] and found that Stacy knew all about it. "Poor Strain," he commended in terms brief in deed, but as strong as

---

[38] Or as, Wassataquoik Stream.

[39] The Crimean War 1853 to 1856.

[40] Lieutenant Isaac Grier Strain led the United States Navy *Darien Exploring Expedition* in 1854 to find an Atlantic to Pacific canal route through the Isthmus of Darién. Although a failed attempt, the Panama Canal was completed in 1914.

New England lips can pronounce. "That Strain," he said, "was a plaguy smart fellow." This was a compliment not to be gainsayed, considering the man it came from. He criticised Strain's course a little, however. "It was unfortunate that he had sailors with him instead of woodsmen. He ought to have left the stream and trusted to his compass;" which is hereby recorded for the benefit of future Darien explorers.

So, walking and halting, we made our pleasant way along, with only the discomfort that no good place presented itself for our noonday rest, until, at two o'clock, we suddenly came out of the thick woods, and the mountain rose before us, "so blue and so far," as Browning says. Another step, and beneath us lay a little lake, as large as Jamaica Pond (near Boston), rippling almost to our feet; close beside us was an old, gray, wooden dam, roughly built years ago by the first lumberers, to flood the brook below at the proper time. Katahdin Lake is the source of the South Branch of the swift Wissaticook, while the North Branch almost encircles, Katahdin. Look in Colton's atlas,[41] and you will find precisely where we were, though the names are not given.

The little waves rippled pleasantly on the yellow beach as we came down upon it, and the sun shone so warmly that we were glad to clamber down into the shade of the old dam, which looked so quiet and gray, that nature seemed to have adopted it as willingly as if beavers had made it, and it did not seem to interfere with that loneliness we loved. The brook slipped through it, and went dashing on, among great rounded rocks, with deep, dark, whirling pools, offering suggestions of

---

[41] J.H. Colton's 1859 Atlas Map of Maine.

superb trout, which it proved hard to fulfill. Among these rocks we perched ourselves, and I afterwards pilfered the following saucy sketch from H.'s pocket book:

"Katahdin Lake, 2 P.M. – Stacy, delighting himself by catching fish in the lake; and McClane delighting us by making a fire to cook them; Alfred, rather dissatisfied with hooks and brooks; Ben, eyeing Katahdin through a spyglass, who eyes him back, quite undisturbed; the rest of the company seeking shade. B. rather sleepy on one side of the dam; C. and Rachel wide awake on the other; Fanny below, letting down her hair over the water, like a bloomerized mermaid; Mary and Theo. trying to balance themselves, in great discomfort, upon a sharp, smooth rock, amid peals of laughter; Kate climbing over similar rocks, in a restless manner, as if she had been cheated of her usual exercise to-day, and meant to make up for it somehow; finally, Alice and H. pledging each other in copious tin cups of cold biscuit and water."

How delighted we were, when it was decided to remain for the night at this pleasant place, catch a liberal supply of fish, and prepare for a laborious walk next day. We were not at all tired, and could easily have gone further; for we had only walked seven miles, though those were forest miles, to be sure. But we all felt stronger and better than when we left home. It only seemed absurd that strong and active women should go anywhere else. I can scarcely look back upon a more blissful memory than that sunny afternoon by the lake; soul and body seemed alike satisfied; trout and tranquility ruled the hour. (N.B. They caught a hundred fish and then stopped.) The freedom of the woods descended deeper and deeper into us, all obstacles seemed removed, and everything looked easier than we had expected.

As for the mountain, nobody can ever imagine how glorious it was that afternoon, changing with the waning sunlight, that sank and faded behind it. The summit was four miles from us in an air-line, and twelve by our track. It was the most personal mountain I had ever seen; more so than Monadnock; far more so, from its isolation, than any of the large family of White Mountains—as, indeed, the abrupt height is much greater—the surrounding country being lower. Alfred compared it to Vesuvius, which he had seen, and we were always impressed with its volcanic appearance. It stood out magnificent and lonely in a sea of woods—square, and jagged at the top; while a projecting shoulder on one side gave us a glimpse of its terrible basin, or crater, whose bare cliffs, one thousand feet high, we could see without a glass. The white "slides" were barer and nearer, and at the foot of one of them, halfway up the mountain, Stacy pointed out our next night's camping-ground. But, after all we had heard of the perpetual clouds and storms, in which this mystic mountain-home of the Indian Pomola[42] was encircled, it seemed strange that it should be so clear and unforbidding now. There was no gorgeous sunset that night, however; but over the whole height there grew a gradual, soft film, and the peak retired further and further away, as if following the light over the western horizon. A few small and placid clouds just lingered round its brow, — reddish, brown, and golden — while the lake below began to be gently ruffled by the evening breeze.

But I think it is time to draw upon a certain epic, which was made by the company on our return, being a veritable history

---

[42] More typically spelled, Pamola. Thoreau had written Pomola.

of our progress. Most of it was written in the steamboat, Rachel acting as scribe, while the other passengers, drawing round, looked on with wonder, and one asked me confidentially, "if that was the young lady who wrote verses for the newspapers."

Here is a specimen:

But now we'll bid our lyre awake,
To sing the glories of the lake.
Beyond it King Katahdin towered,
With sunset glories richly dowered.
The horizon was shrouded with silvery haze,
That ethereal veil of our autumn days;
The travelers wander here and there,
To camp-ground, or to lake repair;
Some catch the fish, some sketch the view;
Workers there are, and idlers, too;
Beneath the dam the latter rest,
Reading aloud, with eager zest,
Those words of our great Emerson,
Which from the winds and waves have won
That harmony of rhyme and rune,
Which chimes with changing nature's tune;
And then the autumn evening long
Was passed in merry games and song.
In the night the loon's laugh, clear and shrill,
Sounded from every echoing hill,
And we heard, above the wild wind's roar,
The tramp of the moose on the forest floor.

That last line means something; it brings me to an adventure, with a preliminary to it. That night as we sat singing, and Kate's rich voice was mounting up in the fine chorus of the "Old Kentucky Home," suddenly, "Hush — a footstep!" cried Fanny, melodramatically, and hush it was. And a footstep it was, too; for, listening intently, we heard the distinct but cautious tread of four feet, receding into the bushes.

"Moose," said McClane, briefly, and explained that our fires were made in a moose path, where they came down to drink. Out went our guide, into the darkness, with a rifle, but came back unsuccessful, though we had heard the rifle crack; and next day we found that the pretty creature had made its way to the water, and refreshed itself, in spite of us. We were glad enough that they did not shoot it, and, as I timidly remarked to C., "Suppose it had been a man, he might have been killed." "Certainly," he coolly replied, "for we knew there was nothing outside but what ought to be killed,"— a rather startling view, and, perhaps, a little exclusive, we thought.

Now for the adventure. "Wakeup, boys, Billy Kirby is going to die," as the Howadji has it.[43] Just as we had got our birch cups and platters ready (for we had them fresh at each meal, and burned them afterwards, the most thorough housekeeping we had ever known), we heard, close to us, **bang! bang!** two rifle shots in quick succession. We looked round, and there lay our private arsenal, against a tree! Who

---

[43] A reference to chapter XV, 'Adventure,' of the book, "The Howadji in Syria," by George William Curtis (1851).

could it be" We had felt as far from men as if we were in the middle of the ocean.

Some cried, "L. has followed us after all," and we all rushed out.

H. and I ran to the lakeside, and there lay the gun, and there stood such a figure — clothes ragged and torn from the woods, face haggard, wild eyes like blue fire, hair dripping from a hasty ablution; he looked intoxicated, or insane, and turned out only sleepless and hungry; a wandering hunter, who had come through on our track from Hunt's, since 2 P.M. the day before, lost his way in the "fathoms five" bog, and had no sleep. Our woodsmen took his measure at a glance, and took him to their hearts at once — we took him to our breakfast. He had partridges for our larder, having had better luck than we, and, moreover, kept us supplied from that moment. He was a Lowell man, but had been to California, and everywhere else; he wore a gay Mexican poncho, and half the time went bareheaded, with elf locks, and keen, metallic blue eyes; and Ben christened him "Mr. Wildfire."

It had rained the night previous, and we feared a wet day; but the mornin was only cold and raw. This showed the mountain in a new aspect of wonder. Instead of that radiant outline of filmy brightness, there was now a vast castle of chill gray cloud, with dark towers of precipice frowning here and there, between. It was no longer our summer friend, but the gloomy and awful abode of Pomola. We remembered what storms others had suffered on that height; and what Thoreau said, that it seemed a slight insult to the gods to climb their mountains; and we shuddered to think that our next night's camp would be within that circle of white, soft, cold, vaporous mystery. Should we dare it? But, moment by moment, clouds went and came, and always more went than came, and at last the sunlight once more shone brightly on the wood fringed lakes, and we went up to breakfast as aforesaid.

That morning we walked four miles to Roaring Brook, and it was exciting enough to know that now we were at the real base of the mountain; here we talked an hour, and while Stacy fried the fish, we sat upon a sturdy pine trunk, which McClane had promptly felled for our bridge, after which the same enterprising person climbed the tallest spruce in the neighborhood, and threw down the topmost spire to us.

After dinner we began to go up in earnest, and sometimes went astray a little, and learned the difference between even "a spotted trail" and the untried forest—not that any path is cleared in either case, but that the former is always a practicable track, and you may be sure it does not end in a swamp, a cliff, or a jungle. Three miles more, and we struck Avalanche Brook, beside whose brink we threw ourselves down, in as much delight as if there were no other water in the world. Indeed, it is no fancy to say, that to sight, taste, and touch, such water is as different from the water of civilization as the snow of Vermont is from the snow of Broadway. It was more than all our previous excitements, to look up through a vista of green woods, and see the bright water bubbling and rushing among white rocks and cliffs, seeming as if a waterspout had just burst in the sky. Up we soon began to go, bounding from rock to rock, now in the water, now out of it, now slipping, now springing, as if our limbs had ceased to be brittle, and the mountain air had transformed us to india-rubber. We went so fast it seemed like flying, and the guides kept checking us. Two miles were passed without knowing it. We came closer and closer into a gorge of the mountain, with glimpses upward of the frowning peak, soon lost again – high walls on each side, and enchanting visions behind us, of miles of level country, all one forest, framed in a foreground of green boughs, or else "great granite jambs," like the highland descriptions in the "Bothie."[44] But we were growing tired, especially during some *detours* through the woods, and it was becoming darker and colder. The wind blew fiercely down from the heights, and our leaders looked a little anxious; more so, when we approached our camping-ground, and heard the report of our returning pioneers; water was far off, the wood was white birch good kindling, but poor fuel-worse yet, the wind blew so that no tent could be raised, and scarcely would the fire burn. And here were we, wet, cold, tired, hungry. But what of that? We rose with the crisis. This was what we had come for; to take nature as she was, and see all sides – we should have been defrauded with only sunshine. So we felt, and so we said, and our companions were bright again instantly, seeing that we were. One thing was instantly settled, to change our ground further into the woods; the gentlemen were all soon set to work, and some of the ladies, too, while some of us dried ourselves as well as we could, with the smoke whirling furiously hither and thither, and often into our very faces, as we sat in our blankets. Soon a brighter flame blazed

---

[44] A bothy (an old alternative spelling was *bothie*), is a small hut or cottage, common in remote mountainous areas of Scotland, Northern England, and Northern Ireland. Higginson may have been referring here to the poem, "The Bothie of Tober-Na-Vuolich - A Long-Vacation Pastoral" by Arthur Hugh Clough. Written in 1848, there are lines which read, "Where in the morning was custom, where over a ledge of granite Into a granite basin..."

at a short distance, and presently came Messrs. C. and B. with great torches of birch bark to light us through the wood. Mr. Wildfire was invaluable, and his partridges delicious; some fish still remained also, and we tried a new method of cooking them, by roasting on sharp sticks before the fire, which proved quite successful. We could not raise our tents, because the smoke shifted every moment, and would have suffocated us; but one tent was spread for a couch for us women folk, above the invariable bed of hemlock, another was securely hung behind us, for a curtain against the furious blast; there was an immense fire, beyond which our companions were dimly seen curled in their shawls or blankets, on mother earth, taking such comfort as they could get. In spite of all our troubles, we had a merry evening. Fanny wandered about a great deal, wrapped in a long blanket, like an insane squaw,[45] and kept turning and arranging a great many pairs of shoes before the fire, as if they were flapjacks. But the rest of us laughed a great deal at her, and at each other, and at anything but dear old Katahdin; and at last we went into a refreshing sleep, and nobody took cold. If we did wake occasionally, it was pleasant to look up, and listen to the young whirlwinds that came blustering down from

---

[45] *Squaw* is the spelling of the Algonquian word *squa*, which means mother, or young wife. For the linguistic misinterpretation in recent decades, see, *Hubbard's Guide to Moosehead Lake and Norther Maine, Annotated Edition.* (Burnt Jacket Publishing, 2020). Here Higginson is referring to Fanny, who in a motherly fashion is concerned with the all-important shoes for their journey, for any woodsman knows, leather footwear left too long near a hot fire will shrink, and be impossible to put on the next morning.

the summit to twist and twirl the tree-tops, and peer down into our place of retreat.

The next morning rose perfectly magnificent. From our dressing-room in a sheltered nook by Avalanche Brook, we looked straight into the sunrise, as it came fresh and gorgeous over the far eastern horizon, and it thrilled a glow of hope all through us, to conquer the chill of that morning air. The mountain peak, which seemed to hang sheer above us, was absolutely cloudless, and shone rosy with answering light. All smiled benignant, and we shivered acquiescent. Our teeth, indeed, chattered, but our hearts bounded; and we went back to our partridges in bliss.

That day was such a day as one dreams of for the great days of history. What had we done to deserve such love from Pomola, when scarcely a previous visitor had seen his home in sunshine? But now it seemed as if every cloud that lingered on the earth's surface was cleared away to the antipodes, and this one bright epoch allotted to Katahdin and to us.

We ran rather than walked, a quarter of a mile through the woods, and came out at the foot of the great slide. Oh! what a place. One broad gray furrow up the mountain side; that was the slide. Fancy a dozen gray walls of crumbling stone, each steeple-high, piled one on the other, up into the sky; that was the mountain. We felt like standing off a little, lest the peak itself should totter over upon our heads. We sat down to meditate. Then we got up, to climb.

All I can say is that we did climb, and got to the top somehow. I have an indistinct recollection that the summit looked about half a mile off, vertically, from the bottom—a mile when half way up — and two miles afterwards; that the ridges, which looked from below near to the summit, looked from above close to the base; that the people above us seemed to be hung on pegs, and the people below us to be balanced upon the tops of trees; that sometimes we were tugged along by gentlemen, and sometimes offered to help gentlemen along; that it was very pleasant to stop and roll stones down, but not quite so pleasant to start again, and drag ourselves up; that finally when we got near the top among the blueberry and cranberry beds, it seemed an absolute embargo on further progress; at least, till we had eaten over the whole berry garden, covering perhaps an acre and a half. But how delicious that long repose was, to cling to the side of the mountain by the bushes (for it really amounted to that), nibble the minute morsels of aromatic nourishment, which the bears had left for us, facing round sometimes, from the berries, to look at the universe. Among this vegetation, grew low and stunted evergreen bushes, that would, we were assured, have been trees further down; but we did not need to clamber over the tops of these, as other explorers had done on a different side of the mountain. On this side it was bare enough, and there was no obstacle but the trifling one of perpendicularity. In our weakness we found that sufficient; but nevertheless, I have an impression, that the first on top was a woman. At any rate, the ascent took three hours.

The top of the mountain can be depicted at a single stroke, to any well instructed woman. Merely fancy the rim of a teacup, five miles round, with a piece broken out of one side. Beside this, the whole is jagged and uneven; nibbled, in truth, by a thousand or two of hungry winters. So that after we had once reached the edge on the southeast, we spent an hour more in climbing a mile further along, higher, and still higher, up one dark, sharp cliff, and down another, with views right and left, and often at liberty to tumble off either way, at our pleasure. Dark, bare, inhospitable, impenetrable granite; if there is anything solid in the material globe, we thought we had found it at last. It was more impressive than the vast pile of broken fragments, which forms the summit of Mount Washington; and it is singular, that though not volcanic, it closely resembles in size, shape, and proportions the only volcanic crater I ever saw.

How strange it was to be lifted, at a gigantic height, with a narrow pedestal beneath one's feet, sheer up into the blue dome of heaven; but very kindly that blue dome received us, so simple in coloring, so sublime; one soft white bar of cloud encircling the whole heavens near the horizon, and nothing else to mar the absolute and perfect hue. Such simplicity of coloring, blue sky, white cloud, and beneath, one sea of green; only, here and there lay noble lakes—scattered fragments of the sky mirror — Milnocket,[46] with its thousand isles, "the crystal Ambijejis,"[47] Chesuncook, and the rest. To the southeast, Lake Katahdin lay delicately couched amid its long, evergreen branches, and we thought that had we wings as eagles we could make one dip into its pale soft waters, and then swoop homeward. The forest trees had not the look of vast size that we expected; but the density was beyond expression. "It did not look as if a solitary traveler had cut so much as a walking-stick there." Only we were startled to see, below us, two faint dimples in the woods at the very base of

---

[46] Current spelling is Millinocket.
[47] Current spelling is Ambajejus.

the mountain. One, Stacy assured us, was where the young trees had been cleared for our last night's camp—another marked a spot where he himself had camped for a longer time. So unconsciously do we leave our mark in the universe. Afterwards they showed us "the farm" — a dot of brighter green in the remote distance — and something white, which they stoutly asserted to be the village of Patten.

Then the basin, or crater, lay on our right, encircled by the vast rim along which we picked our way. It was exciting to hear, that descent into it was absolutely impossible, and it could only be approached by the gap aforesaid on the eastern side. It was exciting to roll stones over precipices, whither even our agile guides could not fellow; and hear the sharp rattle and crash from depth to depth. Yet it did not look bare in that great basin; for its area of two hundred acres is mostly overgrown with bushes, among which, however, great slides track themselves in heaps of desolation, and great square blocks of granite suggest shuddering fancies of the time when, in the dead of winter, perhaps, those giant masses crashed and rebounded from above.

On the south side of this basin, there is a deep, narrow indentation, through which the winds rush fearfully, it is said, when Pomola's cloud factor within is in active operation. This must be passed, and much hard clambering up and down, if we would go still further, and we saw there was one point of rock, some two miles distant, that was somewhat higher than that on which we stood; but we had done enough, fortune had favored us, and why should we tempt her more? We had done it; we had ascended Katahdin, and the reality was more than our dreams.

Only Fanny was dissatisfied; she and Mr. Wildfire wished to go further yet. The latter had heard of a spring of good water two miles ahead, and he wanted "just to step along and try a taste of it." We were quite in a condition to appreciate good spring water, but McClane, with gallant labor, had just brought us a small pailful from nearly that distance in a different direction, and we thought that "just to step along" over two miles of rugged granite cliffs, at a height of six thousand feet, was a step too far. However, there was more reason in his remark than is apparent to those who do not know the taste of mountain springs; and when we saw Mr. W. clamber on before us, through the aforesaid gully, bareheaded, his long hair and poncho waving in the fierce wind, which even then blew there, his gun slung over his shoulder – climbing straight up cliffs where a civilized cat would have lost eight of her lives, and gazing round at us half way, with wild, triumphant eyes, we really felt ashamed not to go where he did, though, I dare say, we should all have been at the north pole by this time, if we had once undertaken to follow. We resisted, brought Fanny back, wrote our names on a paper, and put it in a phial, which Stacy hid somewhere in this corner-stone of the globe; and then resolutely *went* down.

First, however, we came suddenly upon the one inhabitant of the region Pomola's sole incarnation; but here I must draw upon the epic again:

> "Bristling, bouncing, black and big,
> There bolted forth a queer *'quill pig;'*
> He had for one pen the mountain side,
> And a thousand more were stuck in his side.
> Stacy drove him from rock to rock,

With sometimes a poke, and sometimes a
    knock–
Stirring him up with good-will hearty
For the benefit of the stranger party."

One or two halts among the cranberry bushes, on which his hedgehogship (quill-pig is the vernacular) was browsing, and, with a large supply of this valuable addition to our *cuisine*, we stepped over the edge of Katahdin.

That descent was a good deal quicker than the ascent, a little easier, and far more amusing. There is a picture in Punch's "Tour of Brown, Jones, and Robinson," which always recalls it to us.[48] Ben had previously described the place to us, as one "where the shortest jacket would trail on the ground."

THE SAFEST WAY OF COMING DOWN A MOUNTAIN.

Illustration from *The Foreign Tour of Messrs. Brown, Jones and Robinson,* by Richard Doyle (c. 1854).

---

[48] *Punch,* or *The London Charivari,* established in 1841 was a British weekly magazine of humor and satire. The story by Richard Doyle, "The Foreign Tour of Messrs. Brown, Jones and Robinson," included the image as shown, which is likely the one recalled by Higginson.

Down we slid, two and two, supported on canes if we had them, over the steep surface of decomposed granite, often dislodging large stones, which would have damaged those below us, only that the crumbled gravel soon stopped them by its friction. In an hour and a half we accomplished what had cost us three in the morning; and it was pleasant to pause where Avalanche Brook distilled itself — a series of tiny drops — from the shelter of a rock-fragment, in the very middle of the great slide. We could see also the tracks of other brooks in wooded ravines along the mountain, and the scars of other, but smaller, slides.

Before sunset, we had reached our camp of the preceding night. We damsels were allowed to render some aid in stewing the delicious cranberries, of a more sweet and spirited flavor than their lowland cousins, which made a sumptuous sauce for our *toujours perdrix*.[49] Our supply of spoons being limited, we had little wooden ones, clean and pure as our birch-bark platters. It was observed that the "tin cup aristocracy" (which was the obnoxious epithet given to the possessors of those conveniences, all aristocracy, however, being, as Theo. said, "founded essentially on tin," had gradually diminished in number; even the precious cup on which Fanny's initials had been engraved with a jack-knife, disappearing at last in Avalanche Brook. Many, indeed, were the jokes made around that evening's fire (though they were never a rare commodity with us); the glorious weather, the day's enjoyment, the success, the absence of discomfort or accident — all raised our glee to the highest point, and it found vent in words and acts

---

[49] The meaning of *toujours perdrix is:* always partridge, too much of a good thing.

of harmless merriment, which the cold world shall never, never know from me. But poor H. never had such hard work to send us to bed, as that night, though we had a tent over our heads, and no more smoke in our faces than was good for us. At last, however, we all had our eyes shut, and we five slept like the "seven."[50]

Off we plunged, down the brookside, next morning, after the gentlemen had fired at a mark a little, while loiterers were getting ready. The same clear, invigorating morning air, the same merry chase of pure water-drops. As Coeur de Lion, in, "The Talisman," would have given the best year of his life for that one half hour beside the desert spring, so do I now look back upon that foaming water. I remember foreseeing this, as I sat once that morning, all alone, waiting for the others to overtake me — sitting between great masses of rock, rounded smoothly by the crystal stream which poured from one aquamarine basin into another, and looking through a gap of trees upon fair Katahdin Lake, and a soft blue hill beyond it. And yet, I thought, people travel to Scotland and to Switzerland who have never been here, and who have no more personal experience of a hemlock bed than of the bed of the Atlantic.

We crossed Roaring Brook once more, and dined that day by a nameless woodland pond, and at night, our beloved "Lake-camp" received us again after our ten-mile walk, and we called it home. We loved it all the more, because we had a foreboding that it would be our last night in the woods; and so it proved. As Stacy predicted, we easily accomplished, next

---

[50] Possibly a reference to the story of, "Seven Sleepers," a group of youths who were sealed in a cave and slept for 300 years.

day, the thirteen forest miles that had been two days' work before, and did it, warm as the day was, in a style that delighted him. "In fact," he added, "I've been in the woods with a good many young gentlemen, who would have given out before they got to Hunt's to-day, warm as the weather was, too." Even the taciturn McClane expressed his decided satisfaction; and as for Ben, he said: "I've got a little memorandum book; I don't often put anything down in it; but I shall put this day down, sure."

So we crossed the Wissaticook again, this time without accident, and so we once more divided with our feet the great golden-rods and asters, strolling leisurely, staff in hand, through the sunny wood-path, that September afternoon; and so we came to the East Branch once more, out into the open clearing, opposite Hunt's; and there lay the solid farmhouse upon the bank, and there were the whole family out to see; and there was the batteau beached upon the sand, and McClane waiting to paddle us over. In we sprang, the batteau was pushed from the shore, it traversed the swift black current, we were landed opposite, and our life in the woods was over.

I shall make short work of the remainder; how delighted good Mrs. Hunt was that we had done the jaunt more quickly than women had done it before; how strange it seemed to us to sit on chairs again, and use cups and saucers; how delicious were the bread cakes, and the potatoes, and the milk; how gay we all were, till we had to dance at least; how our only minstrel was a wild Irishman, who played and sang "The girl I left behind me," thrumming with his fingers a clattering accompaniment on a dust-pan; how we thought there never was such inspiriting music, and tired each other down with the wildest of Virginia reels before the great kitchen-hearth. This I never can describe, though it was certainly the wildest scene

I ever witnessed, and seemed more like a highland *bothie* than anything in New England. Happily, in this case, the excitement was all teetotal, and came pure from the happiest of happy hearts. That night we slept as well as we could be expected to do, in real beds, and the next day we all went down the Penobscot in two batteaux, and were almost happier than on any previous day, paddled steadily along the smooth swift canal between drooping trees, seeing no human being except a silent man in a birch canoe, and two girls paddling across to their father's clearing. Sometimes, however, coming to rapids where we passengers had to get out, while two in each batteau guided it magically among great rocks and through narrow passages where it seemed no floating thing could pass without shipwreck. Having only three regular voyageurs, H. went as the fourth, and said it was the most exciting thing he ever did, and like standing on the back of the most spirited horse, and he said, also, that it was perfectly superb to see the consummate skill with which McClane, in the bow of the boat, would guide it among white, whirling torrents, and round sharp angles of threatening rock, where it seemed madness to venture. We got, with difficulty, some dinner at a queer little settlement called Nickatow, and the last part of the way was almost dangerous. It grew late, and there were bad shoals and rapids, or "rips" to pass, and both our comrades and our guides were weary; so we rowed races for a stimulus, and composed saucy verses, and hurled them at each other, and at last, when it was quite dark, we glided out upon the deeper waters of the main Penobscot, and soon after were landed beneath over hanging alders, and walked up through a hushed and star-lit lane, mysteriously, into the little village of Mattawamkeag, and to its large and lighted tavern. There we took leave, not without very genuine signs of true regard on both sides, of our friendly and manly guides. There some of our own party, also, must leave us, and hasten on at midnight. We had one last gay evening in our woodland-dress; and there the history of those bright days must close.

After the story comes the moral. We proved the truth of the prediction we overheard, that it would give us "better fun than a trip to Saratogue," and our moral is, that there is more real peril to bodily health in a week of ballroom than in a month of bivouacs.[51] Our health and strength improved from beginning to end, nor did any ill consequence follow.

---

[51] Bivouacs: a temporary camp without tents or cover, used especially by soldiers or mountaineers.

Katahdin
(Editor's Collection)

VIII — Birch Stream

by
Anna Boynton Averill

At noon, within the dusty town
Where the wild river rushes down
And thunders hoarsely all day long,
I think of thee, my hermit stream,
Low singing in thy summer dream,
Thine idle, sweet, old tranquil song.

No noisy mill enslaveth thee,
No dam doth fret thy waters free,
Soft rippling through the woodland shy,
From where the birches lean across
Thy narrow bed of drowning moss
To where the Indian islands lie.

Northward Katahdin's chasmed pile
Looms through thy low, long, leafy aisle,
Eastward Olamon's summit shines;
And I, upon thy shadowy shore,
The dreamful, happy child of yore,
Worship before mine olden shrines.

Again the sultry, noontide hush
Is sweetly broken by the thrush
Whose clear bell rings and dies away
Beside thy banks in coverts deep
Where nodding buds of orchids sleep
In dusk and dream not it is day.

Again the wild cow lily floats
Her golden-freighted, tented boats
In thy cool coves of softened gloom,
O'er shadowed by the whispering reed,
And purple plumes of pickerel weed,
And meadow sweet in tangled bloom.

The startled minnows dart in flocks
Beneath thy glimmering, amber rocks,
If but a zephyr stirs the brake:
The silent swallow swoops, a flash
Of light and leaves with dainty plash
A ring of ripples in its wake.

Without, the land is hot and dim:
The level fields in languor swim,
Their stubble grasses brown as dust:
And all along the upland lanes,
Where shadeless noon oppressive reigns,
Dead roses wear their crowns of rust.

Within is neither blight nor death:
The fierce sun woos with ardent breath
But cannot win thy sylvan heart.
Only the child who loves thee long,
With faithful worship pure and strong,
Can know how dear and sweet thou art.

So loved I thee in days gone by,
So love I yet, though leagues may lie
Between us, and the years divide.
A breath of coolness, dawn and dew,
A joy forever, fresh and true,
Thy memory doth with me abide.

Birch Stream is the dividing line between the towns of Alton, Maine and Argyle, Maine. Birch reaches the Stillwater River and then drains into the Penobscot. Averill was born in the town of Alton and reminisces about her time spent near this stream.

1890s Advertisement

IX — Is Kokadjo Indian?

READERS of Eckstorm will come to understand her exactitude for place names, particularly as they relate to original names bestowed by Native Americans. These names were handed down to her in stories from Indians, who were friends of her, or her father. In, *Exploring the Maine Woods – The Hardy Family Expedition to the Machias Lakes*, her explanations of Nicatowis Lake (Nicatous) and Peskebegat (Lobster Lake) were covered in detail. In this chapter she provides us with the meanings of Kokadjo, and of Bagaduce. Both essays appeared in *Sprague's Journal of Maine History*. The essay on Kokadjo in 1925, and the essay on Bagaduce in 1914.

The Editor of the Journal (*Sprague's Journal of Maine History)* asked this question a year ago in the first issue for 1924, page 54.[52] It happened that I did not see the query until recently.

Kokadjo is Indian, good Abnaki for "Kettle mountain;" but it is not desirable as a name replacing the old, established names of First, Second and Third Roach Ponds. (The act of

---

[52] The question being referred to was, "Is Kokadjo Indian?" (Vol. 13, No. 1, 1925)

March 3, 1913, names a "Fourth Roach Lake" which I cannot identify, unless it means Spencer Pond.)[53]

The real Indian names of Spencer Pond and First Roach Pond were Kokadjeweengwasebemsis and Kokadjeweemgwasebem. If the act wishes to establish Indian names for these ponds, (or lakes, in more modern parlance), it should have taken these names, given on Mr. Lucius L. Hubbard's well-known map and in the vocabulary at the end of his "*Woods and Lakes of Maine.*"

Kokadjo is the name of Little Spencer Mountain, the more westerly of the two Spencer Mountains, and in its present form is not suited to be used as the name of a lake. The word comes from *kok*, kettle, (which is really an English word disguised), and *wadjo*, mountain, (specifically a lone hill). In compounding, we have dropped the sound of the *w*, thus disguising the root. In making the name for First Roach Pond, to this Indian name for the mountain was added *pegwasebem*, lake. The name of Spencer Pond was further adorned with the diminutive *sis*, little, and would better have been written Kokwadjopegwasebemsis, than in the form on the map, that is "Kettle-Mountain Pond."

My objections to the word Kokadjo for these ponds are two: first, that when you are translating an Indian name, you

---

[53] Spencer Pond is not in the chain of ponds along the Roach River, and it would have been an error for the legislature to include that geographically distant pond in the 1913 renaming act. Eckstorm's mention of possibly this *Fourth Roach Pond* being Spencer Pond is only because the legislature names such a place, and Spencer is the pond closest to Kokadjo, the mountain. See inset at the conclusion of the essay for information on the Act of 1913 and the subsequent Act of 1931.

should translate the whole of it, or let it alone; second, that the names Spencer Pond and First Roach Lake were given very long ago in memory of early settlers, who were worthy of this little tribute to their enterprise and fortitude.

I have taken up with Professor William F. Ganong, our best authority upon Indian place-names, the form of the word Kokadjo.

He writes (in part):

"Concerning *kokadjo* I have been very much interested in trying to trace that word back, but cannot get it past Hubbard.[54] I do not think the form *kok-i-wadjo* would be allowable, because so far as I can make out that *i* possessive syllable applies only to animate things. It seems to me wholly probable that the combination is not aboriginal but is a straight translation of Kettle Mountain into Indian, or it may be that the first syllable, *kok*, describes its shape and is applied to a kettle for that reason. I am afraid this is all the light I can throw on that subject."

My own interpretation is that the names given on Mr. Hubbard's map for Spencer and Roach Ponds are very recent. In old times Indians would hardly have designated bodies of water so far removed from the mountain by a reference to the mountain. They needed some word characterizing what they could see when they got to the pond itself; for, having no maps, their names were descriptive word-pictures. There is no look

---

[54] Ganong was an expert on Native American linguistics. Eckstorm collaborated with Ganong, and Ganong also corresponded with Hubbard. The letter referenced here is available in the University of Maine at Orono, Fogler Library archives in the Fannie Hardy Eckstorm letters.

of antiquity about these names for the ponds. However, the name Kettle Mountain, for Little Spencer Mountain, is very ancient and rests upon an immemorial Indian legend.

In the beginning, when Glusgehbeh (the Micmac Glooscap) lived here, teaching men, one day he and his dog found a cow moose and her calf at Moosehead Lake. The cow he killed and left there; she is Kineo, which from the south is supposed to look like a moose lying down. The calf he pursued to the eastward down to Penobscot Bay. As he chased it upon his snow-shoes, to lighten his load he first threw down the kettle he was carrying, which is now *Kokadjo*, Kettle Mountain, and then his pack, which is Big Spencer Mountain. The Indian name for this is *Sabotawan*, the Pack, because to them it resembles the Indian pack, made up by rolling everything in a blanket, with a long strap so passed through the middle that it both drew the bundle tight and served as a lugging band.[55]

The calf moose went down near Northport, and then swam across Penobscot Bay. Glusgehbeh leaped across the bay and the marks of his snow-shoes used to be plainly seen on Dice's Head, Castine. Madagámoosuk, they were called by the Indians. The calf moose he killed on Cape Rosier, and its hind quarters can be seen there today, when the tide is nearing full. Mooseócatchick, the Moose's Rump, is the Indian name. Beside it lies Osquoón, the Liver. The entrails of the moose Glusgehbeh threw to his dog, and they may be seen, wind and water giving a view of the bottom, trailing all the way across

---

[55] A picture of these mountains is included in this edition.

to Islesboro (where they appear a half mile below Ryder Cove[56]), thence to the western shore of the bay.

The Spencer Mountains
Kokadjo, Little Spencer, The Kettle, on the left.
Sabotawan, Big Spencer, The Pack, on the right.
(*Editor's Collection*)

The meat Glusgehbeh took up on the Bagaduce River and cooked a part of it for himself in a pot-hole in the ledge near the tide-falls above Castine. The dog started to dig a kettle for himself nearby, but being admonished that a dog should eat his food uncooked, that pot-hole is incomplete.

This story I had from aboriginal sources. Thoreau makes a reference to Kineo as once being a moose; Vernon Quinn's "Beautiful America" has an allusion to it and Joseph Necolar's "The Red Man" tells the tale of killing the calf moose. I am not aware that the entire story has been told before this. But the name Kokadjo is thus fully accounted for, though on the face of it the word looks spurious.

It may be added that nothing now would be gained by trying to restore to the mountains known as Big and Little

---

[56] On the east side of North Islesboro.

Spencer, the names which the legend shows belonged to them properly and from remote days. One of these names the Act of 1913 has appropriated and applied to several bodies of water so situated that, in the exigencies of Indian geography, it probably did not belong to any of them, or at most to only one of them. The names of old settlers have been stripped from the places they had held for a century. And nothing has been done except to call some ponds "lakes." Certainly, the Upper Roach Ponds are not lakes, and it is worse to call them lakes than it was for the early settlers to call the lower one a "pond," as they always did.

Yes, Kokadjo is Indian, but the Act of 1913 has made a joke of it.

Fannie Hardy Eckstorm
Brewer, Maine, Feb. 12, 1925.

Maine Act of 1913

Eckstorm mentions the Act of 1913 twice in her essay on Kokadjo. In 1913, the Maine legislature renamed the Roach ponds to the names Ecktorm mentioned in the essay, of Kokadjo Lakes.

And in true government fashion, and not just because if you reverse the 13 in 1913, you get 1931, but the Eighty-Fifth Legislature in the year of 1931, repealed Chapter 64 from 1913, and issued a new law, which brought the names of the lakes full circle back to the pre-1913 act. This change made map makers ecstatic from the easy revenue.

In complete irony, even though Eckstorm pointed out the missing Fourth Roach Pond in her 1925 letter, the legislature, continued to insist on the existence of this pond in 1931.

The map consulted by Eckstorm in 1913 would have been Hubbard's 1899 map. (This is known based on her writing and the note of her map study added in the newly released *Annotated Edition* of *Hubbard's Guide to Moosehead Lake and Northern Maine*.) On the map, Hubbard included the First, Second, and Third Roach Ponds.

Likewise, the map created for Thomas S. Steele, also did not label a 4th Roach Pond. It is not like a pond in that area didn't exist, it is more likely because of the connected waterway, they included the body of water between Trout Pond and 3rd Roach Pond as *part of* 3rd Roach.

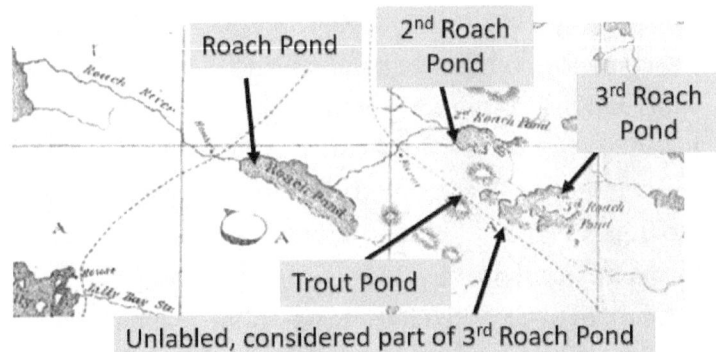

Thomas S. Steele 1881 Map – Area of Roach Ponds

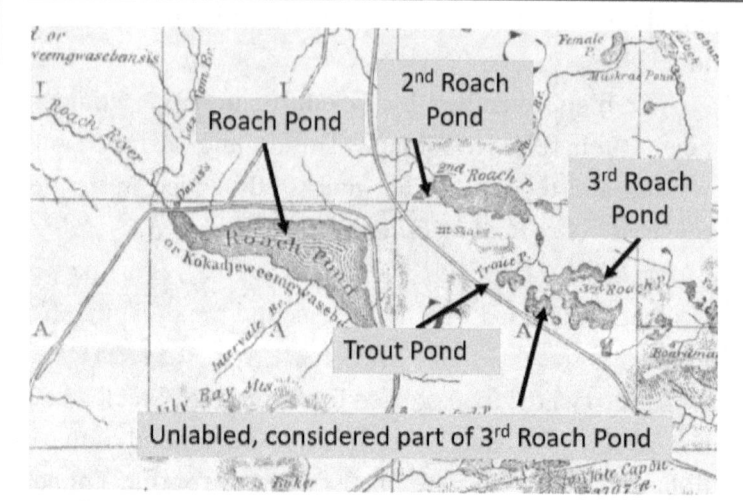

Hubbard's 1899 Map – Area of Roach Ponds

The linguistic question on the Native American name Hubbard applied to First Roach Pond, Kokadjeweemgwasebem, by both Eckstorm and Ganong arose because this waterbody is far removed from Kokadjo, Kettle Mountain. In any event, for now at least, it appears the name Roach and the designation as ponds is here to stay. The origin to the Roach name has been lost, but it is thought to be related to an early settlement.

A modern-day search using an online mapping tool may label the *"unnamed pond"* on the early maps as 4th Roach Pond. It may have been the legislatures had a map that Eckstorm was not aware of, or somewhere along the way, the waterway connecting 3rd Roach and the unnamed pond considered to be part of 3rd Roach, was named as 4th Roach Pond. The Sixth, and Seventh Roach ponds were named later. You might ask, where is 5th Roach Pond? The fifth pond in the sequence is non-existent in the Roach chain.

This is not the only chain of ponds (or lakes) in Maine where the fifth is skipped in the naming. There is an old woodsmen's joke, "there is no fifth pond, for the lumbermen would have drank it, if it were there."

The 1913 Act:

ACTS AND RESOLVES

OF THE

SEVENTY-SIXTH LEGISLATURE

OF THE

STATE OF MAINE

1913

Chapter 64.

An Act to Change the Name of Roach River, First Roach Pond, Second Roach Pond, Third Roach Pond and Fourth Roach Pond, in Piscataquis County.

Be it enacted by the People of the State of Maine, as follows:

Section 1. The name of Roach river, in Piscataquis county, is hereby changed to Kokadjo river.

Section 2. The name of First Roach Pond, in said county, is hereby changed to First Kokadjo lake.

Section 3. The name of Second Roach pond, in said county, is hereby changed to Second Kokadjo lake.

Section 4. The name of Third Roach pond, in said county, is hereby changed to Third Kokadjo lake.

Section 5. The name of Fourth Roach pond, in said county, is hereby changed to Fourth Kokadjo lake.

Approved March 4, 1913.

The subsequent reversal:

Private and Special Laws

OF THE

STATE OF MAINE

As Passed by the Eighty-Fifth
Legislature

1931

Chapter 62.

AN ACT to Change the Names of Certain Waters in Piscataquis County.

Be it enacted by the People of the State of Maine, as follows:

Sec. 1. P. & S. L., 1913, c. 64, **repealed.** Chapter sixty-four of the private and special laws of nineteen hundred thirteen is hereby repealed.

Sec. 2. Certain waters renamed. The names of the following waters in Piscataquis County are hereby changed, as indicated below.

1. The name of Kokadjo river is hereby changed to Roach river.

2. The name of First Kokadjo lake is hereby changed to First Roach pond.

3. The name of Second Kokadjo lake is hereby changed to Second Roach pond.

4. The name of Third Kokadjo lake is hereby changed to Third Roach pond.

5. The name of Fourth Kokadjo lake is hereby changed to Fourth Roach pond.

Approved March 20, 1931.

In this next letter, Eckstorm clarifies yet another Native American place name, that of the Bagaduce. The Bagaduce River is in Hancock, County. A unique natural area, the Bagaduce Falls are reversing falls in the section between Snow Cove and the river's estuary.

Bagaduce

"Notes on Colonial Penobscot" in this Journal (*Sprague's Journal of Maine History*), number 1, volume 1, bring up the name of Begarduce, its origin and meaning. The forms Bagaduce, Matchebignatus, Maja-bagaduce, Biguyduce, Bigayduce, Baggadoose and others are recorded and there seems as yet no authorized form of the word and no settled opinion as to its meaning. In the journal referred to, Judge Williamson is noted as saying that it "might have been derived from Marchebagaduce, which he considers as an Indian word meaning "No good cove;" but he also asserts that it was named for a French officer, Major Bigayduce.

This mythical "major" appeared elsewhere among our ancestors' attempts to adopt Indian names. I have heard old people speak of Major Hindoo; but what they meant was *marjee honta*, the evil spirit. The Indians often used it as an exclamation precisely equivalent to "The Devil!" and the settlers took it in a corrupted form and used it in the same way as an expletive, only they said "Major Hindoo!" Our Major Bigayduce came about in a similar way.

My father, the late Manly Hardy, used to cruise much with the Penobscot Indians along the coast, and he was told by them that Marge-bagaduce (by any spelling preferred) meant "a bad landing place for canoes." It referred to the shore at Castine, exposed to the open sea and in those days covered with rocks and boulders which have since been cleared away. As a birch canoe was as fragile as an eggshell, this roughness of the shore was dreaded by the Indians and so gave the place its name.

I would also call attention to the fact that the road which passes through Holden, past the Town Hall and so up over the Hart Hill, was the old road to Castine and is still often called the Baggaduce Road.[57] The name, in my youth, was especially applied to about a mile of the road between the Town Hall and the Gilmore settlement and would be quite inexplicable were it not understood as a survival in a fragment only of a name once of much wider application.

— Fannie Pearson Hardy Eckstorm
Brewer, Maine — March 12, 1914

Editor's Note: There have been other explanations for this word. Another spelling is Matchebiguatus, taken to mean a place where there is 'no safe harbor.' Other references note the meaning as, 'big tide river.' Wheeler writes, "there is a Penobscot story of the upsetting of a canoe full of Indians, that caused great sorry and distress, and hence the word is thought to signify, "a place of sorrow." The interested reader can find additional information in, "History of Castine, Penobscot, and Brooksville, Maine," by George Augustus Wheeler, 1875 (available on the internet). Eckstorm's main purpose was to relay what the Penobscot Indians told her father directly.

---

[57] A small stretch of road in Holden still goes by the name, Bagaduce Road.

X — Below The Beeches In The Forest Old

by
Anna Boynton Averill

Below the beeches in the forest old
The yellow leaves are strown, and overhead
From sunny boughs a mellow light is shed,
And we together walk the streets of gold.
Across the blue the sunset clouds unrolled,
Pour down pure color till the ways we tread
Are glorified, and eye and soul are fed
With mystic light and splendors manifold.
O, Friend! Is Heaven fairer? Could we see
Into the soul of This that wraps us here,
Were it not one with Heaven's mystery?
O, Earth divine! If we with spirit ear
Could catch the key-note of thy harmony,
Would not the meaning of the whole be clear?

Below the Beeches
(Editor's Collection)

XI — The Legend of Kineo — 1851

MANY of Maine's mountains are still known by the names given to them by the Native Americans, as told to the white explorers, albeit in some cases with altered spelling due to translation. Thoreau and Hubbard were two of the historians of Indian place names in the north woods who did the best documenting of this early history. However, some mountains have been renamed for one reason or another. Near Moosehead, examples are Big and Little Spencer Mountains, for which the names Sabotawan and Kokadjo are rarely known today, and the name change of Big Moose Mountain, which was covered in a prior book.[58] The original names of these mountains were often associated with Indian legends, told to those exploring or being guided through the woods. Since the legends were told and documented by numerous people, during the 1700s and 1800s, there appears to be validity to the stories, even with slight variations.

Mt. Kineo is also named on the basis of legends, two of which were covered in Hubbard books.[59] The following is a third account of the Kineo legend written by E. Oakes Smith. This is the same Smith who was mentioned in the earlier Higginson essay, of the first party of women to summit Mt. Katahdin. Smith wrote this article in 1851, in which she had

---

[58] Hubbard's Guide to Moosehead Lake and Northern Maine (Annotated Edition), Burnt Jacket Publishing (2021).
[59] See note 1, and Woods and Lakes of Maine (Annotated Edition), Burnt Jacket Publishing (2021).

noted that her climb of Kineo was also with the first party of women to have made the summit of that mountain.

In this version of the Kineo legend, she credits the Indian guides with being great storytellers. She specifically mentions that the Indians never pronounce the name *Katahdu*, based on their belief that the mountain is the home to the Spirit of Evil. Katahdu is yet another spelling of Katahdin, and from the earlier essay on the Katahdin legends from Eckstorm, Katahdin as the mountain, was not considered one in the same with the storm-bird Pamola.

In the Smith version, there are several small differences from the one included in the Hubbard book. Based on the oral telling of the legends, and the two versions being originally published some thirty-three years apart, this is understandable. Here, the name, Maquaso is given to mean, "the robin." The courter of Maquaso is spelled as, Muchaé (also as Mackae), and the battle of the tribes for which Kinneho is the hero, is told differently. This version also notes Kinneho as being a chief of his tribe. Other versions do not have him as a chief, but rather the tribe had banished him, even though re returns later and assists them in the winning of a great battle. Smith refers to the Indian pipe, or ghost plant,[60] as originating from the tears of Maquaso; whereas other versions attribute the plant to the tears of Kinneho. Near the end, Smith makes reference to Kinneho being confined to the bowels of the mountain. This may be related to the reference of Kinneho traveling to Katahdin, where it is thought he made a compact with the evil powers there. This pact may have been what his

---

[60] Monotropa uniflora - Indian Pipe, Ghost Flower, or Ghost Plant.

tribe believed that allowed Kinneho to pass into the mountain itself. Such a thought is consistent with Clara Neptune's story to Fannie Eckstorm, in that Katahdin lived within his mountain. Despite these small detail differences, overall, the writings are similar in the story.

Smith also wrote this of the mountain where Maquaso made her lodge: "Squaw Mountain, of which we have before spoken,[61] rises at the distance of five miles from Kinneho. The Indian appellation is lost, and the name it now bears, uncouth as it sounds, was given it by the whites in the first settlement of the country." This naming was based on the legends told about the mountain to the whites.

Reprinted here is the legend written by Smith as relayed to her from the Indian guide who was camping with her party at the top of Mt. Kineo.

---

[61] Earlier in her writing, Smith mentions, "far to the left appeared what is quaintly called Squaw Mountain." Her meaning in the second mention, in using 'uncouth' for the name, would have been referring to the meaning as *in art or language*, as lacking sophistication or delicacy. Given Smith had an appreciation for the Native American names, the lost Indian name for the mountain, which would have been considered to have specific character, is a disappointment to her. Maybe, Mount Maquaso would have been more appropriate than Squaw, and certainly that would have been more fitting than Big Moose Mountain, which obscures the legend and history completely.

"Kinneho: A Legend of Moosehead Lake,"
from Godey's Lady's Book (March, 1851)

"We are in the pathway of Kinneho, when he used to visit yonder," he at length said, pointing in the direction of Katahdu. He saw we were all eager for the story, and he went on; but I must give it in my own words.

The whole way from Moosehead Lake to the base of Katahdu is threaded by a chain of lakes, through which the Indian paddles his canoe, and at the several portages shoulders his light burden till a tramp of a mile, it may be less or more, enables him to launch it once more upon one of these lovely sheets of water. It will be seen that the great promontory which rises out of the centre of Moosehead takes its name from the principal personage of our story.

More than two hundred years ago, an old chief, who had taken a young wife late in life, became the father of a very beautiful girl, of rare wisdom, likewise, whom he called Maquaso, or the robin, because her cheek showed the red through the olive hue, like the feathers upon the breast of this bird. Now this chief, besides being old, was nearly blind. It was believed his young wife had rubbed his eyes while he slept with the leaves of the poisonous hemlock, in revenge for some wrong she had suffered.

Be that as it may, Maquaso, as she came to womanhood, was known to esteem her mother but lightly, while her whole soul seemed devoted to the comfort of her infirm parent. It could not be otherwise but the graces of Maquaso would win the admiration of her people, and we find skins and venison, trophies of the chase and river, were often laid at the door of the wigwam as testimonies of love; but the presents of Muckaé (black heart) far outshone all others. Moreover, whenever the morning showed a heap at the lodge of the old chief, bearing the totem or mark of the young donor, Muckaé spurned it aside with his foot and placed his own offering within the entrance, in a manner that showed it must not be rejected. Maquaso shuddered as she saw this; for Muckaé was a bad man, whom the tribe feared; but he was at the head, and no one dared resist him. When, at length, Muckaé asked her of her father, she made no resistance, but became his wife.

Shortly after this event, her father died, and Maquaso, out of dread of her husband, dissembled her grief for him just as she did her aversion to Muckaé. But, as moons wore on, she grew more stately in manner, and more firm and violent in speech, till the bad chief in time grew half fearful in his turn. She was diligent, patient, and thrifty; his wigwam the best provided amongst the tribe; but Muckaé was morose and cruel of heart, and never a smile beamed from his face. Maquaso spread the skins and cooked his venison, but she was silent; and when the women of the tribe assembled at their feasts of the hunt and ripening corn, she was not among them.

At length, she became the mother of a boy, whom she called Kinneho. Now her whole nature was roused into action. She bathed his limbs, she trained him to courage, to hardihood, and virtue. She taught him to bend the bow, for she had often brought down game for her infirm father. With her own hand she prepared him for the chase or the battlefield, and was never happy away from his side. Kinneho was, in truth, so beautiful, that he seemed worthy of her care. Stately in height and swift of foot, with his mother's clear and vigorous intellect, he soon became first in the war party, as he had always been first in the chase. At the council fire, too, Maquaso, seated with the women, saw with delight that old men listened to his voice with deference, and often followed his suggestions.

She was still beautiful; for, rejecting the servile life that uncultured woman submits to, she had dwelt in the midst of her own great thoughts while her hands labored in the wigwam, therefore care and age had found no place upon which to leave their traces. Her husband had long since given himself up to a morose and solitary life, under pretence of having become a great medicine-man, leaving the whole care of providing for the boy to his mother.

Now whether there is that in human nature that makes it ungrateful to tenderness, regardless of what is lavishly bestowed, and covetous of that which is denied it, or whether there is a depth beyond human requital, we will not take upon ourselves to determine; it may be that moral qualities are transmissible to a greater degree than we comprehend. Whatever might be the cause, Maquaso was stung to the soul to find, as years grew upon the boy, he was morose, cruel, and sullen of heart as his father had been, rewarding her tenderness with scorn or indifference. She was far too wise and too proud to complain at this; but the women, who are always observant of each other, became aware of the fact, and it was much talked about amongst the people. At length, one morning beside the stones of the council fire was found a pair of worn moccasons, a decayed robe, and a braid of hair, which were known to have belonged to Maquaso.

These tokens were designed to indicate that the owner was dead to the tribe; and when it was found that Maquaso had disappeared, terrible thoughts grew upon the minds of the people. It was in vain that Kinneho joined in the search, and declared he was ignorant of her fate; his former bad repute fixed suspicion upon him, and a council was held, before which he was cited to appear. Prior to this, the young men had refused to join him in the hunt, and he was forbidden to sit amongst the chiefs who deliberated upon a war path about to be taken against a party of their enemies who had encamped upon the river Androscoggin.

When Kinneho appeared before the council, the chiefs, one and all, arose and turned their backs upon him. The oldest man amongst them approached him, and taking the war-club from his hand tossed it into the midst of the flames, then seizing his bow, he broke it asunder. Kinneho uttered a cry of rage and defiance, and plunged into the forest.

The chiefs now started on their war-path; but they missed the courage and zeal of Kinneho. The way was long and toilsome, their enemies fierce. As they approached the vicinity, the scouts came in, declaring the numbers of their foe to be many as leaves of the trees, for they counted as many as a dozen smokes. Cautiously did the party come on, watching each the planting of his foot, lest the crackling of a twig or the stirring of a branch should betray their proximity. As they neared, a single voice arose, clear and strong, singing the chant that betokens victory. They uttered the yell of the savage and sprang forward upon the foe. There was a dead silence, and every man stood in the glare of the flame arrested and silent.

The ground was strewn with the dead, and the reeking blood bubbled amid the ashes. Standing above the field of carnage was Kinneho, stringing the the scalps to his girdle. He had kindled fires around the foe, which deceived and bewildered them, and then rushing upon them while they slept, had made them his prey. The young warriors set up a shout of approval, but Kinneho stalked forth in silence, leaving them to the feast of the dead.

At length, he fixed his lodge upon the top of the mountain in the centre of Moosehead Lake, which still bears his name. Here the tribe, in their hunts, saw all night the light against the sky, and a long streak of red across the water; but no one dared to approach him. If by chance a party met him in the forest, they fled before him; for he was known to be implacable in his rage, and the wildest stories were told of his single-handed valor.

Soon after Kinneho had established himself upon Moosehead, he observed a faint gleam of fire upon what is now called Squaw Mountain. At first, he thought this might be a tree blasted by lightning slowly consuming itself; but as night after night presented the same appearance, he resolved to learn the mystery. Perhaps he hoped to surprise a party of his people. He crossed the lake in his canoe, and drawing it up under the bank, followed the direction in which he had seen the light. He ascended the mountain with covert step; as he neared the top, he saw beside a small spring that bubbled from the rocks a rude lodge. As he stood gazing upon the scene, a woman came from the door bearing a birchen bowl, which she filled at the fountain. It was the once beautiful Maquaso, bent, emaciated, and her hair bleached to the color of the hoar frost. Kinneho rushed forward and clasped her in his arms. She looked in his face; but her eyes were wild and streaming with tears. Kinneho smoothed the white hair from her brow and strove to comfort her; but she seemed not to know him, only weeping and wringing her hands. He brought down a partridge with his bow and spread it upon the coals, in the hope it might restore her; but she only wept the more, with her eyes fixed piteously upon his face. At length they closed slowly—Maquaso was dead.

Kinneho made her grave beside the fountain, and came piously day by day with fruits and venison to comfort her in the long journey to the spirit-land. It was to *the tears of Maquaso that we owe one of the most beautiful of our August plants. Wherever these fell, the Indian pipe appeared, white and pure, like congealed sorrow.* The Great Spirit caused this to spring up as a memorial of her grief.

Kinneho lived more than a hundred suns in this desolate spot. His people tried to conciliate him; but he would never return to their favor. Once a year, when the Gat-gwah-da-ah, or Watchers, as the Indians beautifully term the Pleiades,[62] hung at evening in the west, he went across the chain of lakes to the Great Mountain, or Katahdu. Why he did so, how he dared to do so, no one knew; but old men believed he had made a compact with the evil powers there; but for what purpose is now lost.

At length, his fire appeared no more upon the top of the mountain. Hunters, as they peered through the trees at the marge of the lake, could no more see him, as they often had done, moving to and fro upon the bold cliff. They told how Kinneho never bent with age, how his white hair and eagle eye looked venerable, yet terrible, as he stood taller than other chiefs, and striking terror into their hearts. When they had watched night after night, and were sure he was not there, they ventured to cross the lake, thinking to find him dead in his lodge.

---

[62] A star cluster also known as The Seven Sisters.

But neither chief, nor lodge, nor vestige of any kind rewarded their search. There is a fountain welling from the side of the rock; here they thought at least to find a pipe, a bowl, or something to show that human life had been passed in so wild a spot; but the redberries clustered then, as now, above the clear water, and all was solitary and token-less.

Men remembered the visits of Kinneho to the Great Mountain (Kathadin), and shook their heads bodingly; and when it was found that the top of the cliff was covered with flinty rocks, as if they had been melted in the fire, that neither grass nor moss grew where the footsteps of the man passed, they were confirmed in their worst suspicions. They believed the stones were burned and melted under the feet of the necromancer, Kinneho, who is now confined in the bowels of the mountain.

— E. Oakes Smith (1851)

XII — Kineo

KINEO
THE LEGEND OF MOOSEHEAD LAKE
by
Frances Laughton Mace
from Legends, Lyrics and Sonnets (1883)

How beautiful the morning breaks
Upon the King of mountain lakes!
The forests, far as eye can reach,
Stretch green and still from either beach,
And leagues away the water's gleam
Resplendent in the sunrise beam;
Yet feathery vapors, circling slow
Wreathe the dark brow of Kineo.

The hermit Mount in sullen scorn
Repels the rosy touch of morn,
As some remorseful, lonely heart,
From human pleasure set apart,
Shrinks even from the tender touch
Of pity, lest it yield too much,
So speechless still to friend or foe,
Frowns the black cliff of Kineo.

Yet, as the whispering ripples break
From the still surface of the lake
On the repellent rocks, they seem
To murmur low, as in a dream,

The mountain's name, and day by day
The listening breezes bear away
A memory of the long ago.,
A sad, wild tale of Kineo.

How many moons can no man say
O'er heaven's blue sea have sailed away,
Since Kineo and his fleet canoe
First vanished from his kindred's view.
Hunter and warrior, lithe and keen,
No brave on all the lake was seen
Whose wigwam could such trophies show,
As the green roof of Kineo.

But wrathful, jealous, quick to strife,
He lived a passion-darkened life;
Even Maquaso, his mother, fled
His baneful lodge in mortal dread.
Then gathering round the midnight fire,
The old men spake with threatenings dire
"Out from our councils he must go,
The demon-haunted Kineo!"

In sullen and remorseful mood
He gave himself to solitude.
Up the wild rocks by night he bore
Of all he prized a stealthy store, —
Flint, arrows, knife and birch. Who knows
But some dark lock or dead wild rose,
The phantom of an untold woe,
Shared the lone haunt of Kineo?

The mountain was his own; than he
None other dared its mystery.
None sought to meet the savage glare
Of the wild hunter in his lair:
But when far up the mountain side
Each night a lurid flame they spied,
The watchful red men muttered low,
"There hides our brother Kineo."

Years passed. Among the storm-swept pines
From moon to moon he read the signs
Of blossom and decay. He knew
The eagle that familiar flew
About his path. The fearless bird
His melancholy accents heard,
But glen or shore no more might know
The swift, still step of Kineo,

Save once. His tribe in deadly fray
Had battled all the lowering day,
And many a brave Penobscot's blood
Was mingling in the lake's pure flood,
When like a spectre, through the gloom,
With gleaming knife and eagle plume,
And glance that burned with lurid glow,
Strode the bold form of Kineo!

A hush like death — and then a cry,
Fierce and exultant, pierced the sky!
They rallied round that fiery plume
And smote the foe with hopeless doom.

But when the grateful warriors fain
Would seek his well-known face again,
Their gifts and homage to bestow,
Gone, like a mist, was Kineo.

They saw him not, but from that hour
They bowed before his wizard power;
His watch-fire grew to be a shrine
Half terrible and half divine.
None ever knew when death drew nigh,
When into darker mystery
Of cloud above or deep below
Stole the sad ghost of Kineo.

But when his camp-fire burned no more,
The solitary mountain bore
His name; and when at times the sky
Grew dark, a long, despairing sigh
Down the dark precipices rolled
And tempest terrible foretold.
The fishers feared the wind, the snow,
The lightning, less than Kineo.

Now beautiful the morning skies
Look on this forest paradise;
Fresh voices, loud and joyous, wake
The echoes of the grand old lake:
But underneath that frowning height
The shadow and the spell of night
Come back: the oars fall still and slow,
The waves sigh, Peace to Kineo!

XIII — Xsébem' - Moosehead Lake

IN 1926, Fannie Hardy Eckstorm contributed an article to *Sprague's Journal of Maine History.* analyzing the "1764 Chadwick Survey of Maine." Eckstorm references Chadwick's journal in which he wrote the name of what is now Moosehead Lake as, "Moose Hills Lake." The rough depiction of the lake on his map was labeled, Lake Sebem. Eckstorm concludes this reference to "Moose Hills Lake" was with regards to Kineo and the two Spencer mountains. This is assuredly related to the legend of Glusgehbeh as written in the earlier chapter. Such naming is consistent with the 1761 map from Montresor, with the lake as, "Moose-Deer Lake," and "Lac Orignal" and Kineo as, "Mount Orignal."[63]

While the legend of Glusgehbeh identifies the shape of Kineo as a, 'stooping moose,' it is possible the change from Moose Hills to Moosehead was based on a map makers translation of the story. It has also been noted that the naming could have changed to Moosehead based on the lake being the headwater of the Kennebec River. The labeling as 'Moose Head' (written as two words) was used as early as 1795 on Osgood Carleton's map. However it occurred such a name referencing a moose is a departure from the name and meaning given to the lake by the Native Americans.

---

[63] On this map, the English and French languages are out of order and the labeling should have been, "Moose-Deer Lake," and, "Lac Orignal." Orignal being French for moose.

Montresor's Map ~ 1761

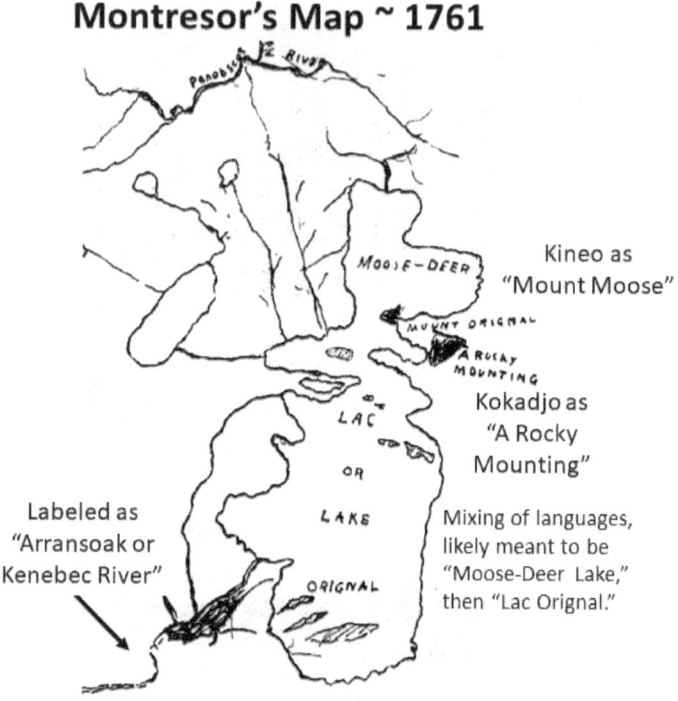

Kineo as
"Mount Moose"

Kokadjo as
"A Rocky
Mounting"

Labeled as
"Arransoak or
Kenebec River"

Mixing of languages,
likely meant to be
"Moose-Deer Lake,"
then "Lac Orignal."

Documented names for the lake in the late 1700s took the form of, Keseben, likely from, K'chi-sebam, meaning "the big lake," with other spellings as Sebaim or K'sebem. The derivation is the same as Maine lakes Sebago and Sebec, with the meaning of, 'wide extent of water.' Lucius Hubbard noted during the 1800s that the Augusta Land Office had used the names Seboumook, Sebaumock, Seeboumock, and Seboumock all referring to Moosehead Lake. The Penobscot Indians who populated the region called the lake Xsebem. The Abnakis referred to the waterway as Sebamook.

The map history shows that by the 1850s the name Moosehead was being applied to the lake. This occurred before an accurate outline for the lake had been drawn; an outline which certainly resembles the head of a moose. Thus, the naming of the lake as 'Moosehead,' was independent of an accurately drawn outline.

From Carleton's 1795 Map

Around 1870, John Way, arrived in Greenville with ideas of drawing the most detailed map of the north woods. His story is told in, "Paddle and Portage — from Moosehead Lake To The Aroostook River Maine."[64] Way's map of 1874 depicted the most accurate outline of Moosehead Lake and preceded Hubbard's first edition.

Eckstorm summed up her analysis with, "When the name of 'Moosehead Lake' came in I do not know, nor why. Apparently, it was transferred from the names of the mountains nearby."

---

[64] A book by Thomas Sedgwick Steele. The story is also included in the two-book edition of Steele's memoirs, "Thomas S. Steele's Maine Adventures," (Burnt Jacket Publishing (2021), and includes additional information about John Way.

However it happened, isn't it serendipitous that the final drawn shape is reflected in the name that was bestowed on this wonderful waterbody?

— Tommy Carbone (2021)

John Way Jr.'s 1874 Map
Moosehead Lake area.
(Dark line around the lake has been added for illustration.)

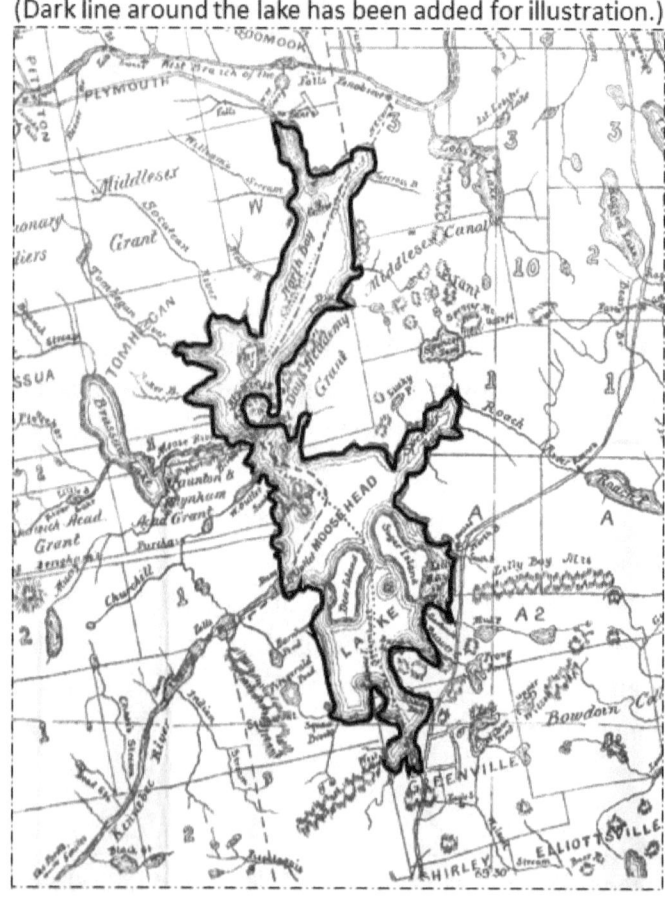

XIV — Panthers in Maine

THE Canada lynx and bobcat, based on internet posts, game cameras, and the editors' own sightings in the woods around Moosehead Lake, are either thriving more than ever, or people with cameras are now out-of-doors more often in the same areas these animals have always been. A few years ago, a video on the internet captured two Canada lynx, in the middle of the road to Rockwood, Maine, hissing and screaming at one another. Whether one would not let the other cross the road, or some other turf war was happening, we do not know, but the cats paid no attention to the vehicle or the cameras rolling. While these large cats are prevalent, as far as the editor knows, no videos or photographic evidence has surfaced of the panther being in Maine. The subject of panthers, or mountain lions, roaming the state has been debated for well over a hundred years.

The following is a letter written to the editors of *Forest and Stream* in 1901 by a C. H. Ames, with a request for information on the once, or then current existence of panthers living in Maine. The article was titled, *No Panthers in Maine*. The editors of *Forest and Stream* contacted Manly Hardy, who was a frequent contributor to the magazine. Hardy responds to the letter based on his extensive experience trapping throughout the northeast, and from his fur trading business where he bought and sold across the United States, Canada, and around the world.

Boston, Mass., Jan. 4. — *Editor Forest and Stream*:

I would like to raise the question whether the true North American panther has ever been killed or seen in the State of Maine. My own belief is that it has not been. I know that the papers of Maine often contain thrilling accounts of people being pursued by panthers, of their blood-curdling cries having been heard, their long, tawny bodies and waving tails having been fairly seen and fully identified, etc., yet I have reason to think that in every instance where the supposed panther was really seen or heard the real animal was nothing nearer to the panther than the well-known Canada lynx or the equally well-known wildcat or bobcat. Why the panther should not occur in Maine I have no idea. I have the impression that the animal has been killed in Vermont, and even within recent years, and I believe that that most scrupulously exact writer, Rowland E. Robinson, described in one of his more recent stories, published in Forest and Stream, the shooting of one in Vermont.

If there is an authentic record of one having been killed in Maine I should much like to hear of it. Is the skin of one killed there anywhere preserved?

Mr. Manly Hardy, the well-known naturalist, and for fifty or more years past the most extensive fur buyer — as I suppose — east of the Rocky Mountains, at any rate of New England and a large portion of the adjoining Provinces, tells me that he has never handled the skin of a panther killed in Maine.

The nearest I can come to what seems an authentic account of panthers in Maine is the testimony of my old guide and valued friend. T. W. Billings, of Brownville. Mr. Billings has more than once told me of the occurrence. He was when a young man hunting and trapping in the extreme northern part of Maine, and one day — from a hill which commanded a view of the frozen surface of a lake — he saw two large animals, which he unhesitatingly took to be panthers, come out upon the ice and play. He described their lithe movements and their leaping over one another, and I think he spoke of their waving tails — though on this point I cannot now be sure. Billings took to hunting and trapping at a very early age, and rapidly acquired the skill for which he was noted, and I should suppose that at the time mentioned he must have been entirely familiar with both the Canada lynx (or, as he would have called it, the *lucivee*) and the bobcat. I remember well his description of their great size and strength, and his frank confession that he was quite willing to observe them at a safe distance, and to pursue his hunting in another direction.

But if even a very few of the modern Maine panther stories are true, someone must at some time, have killed one of the animals, and we shall have the skin in evidence. We know how the recent stories of wolves in Maine "peter out," and either turn out to be altogether myths or the animal proves to be a yellow dog. There is big game in Maine "for sure," but I am inclined to think it does not now include the wolf, and that it never included the panther. Still, I should be interested to find myself proved or mistaken.

Just here, also, I would like someone to tell me what animal was meant by the "leurxsus" or "Indian devil." Till recent years I supposed it must be the panther — but now suppose it must be either the *lucivee* or the bobcat.

— C. H. Ames.

Editor Response:

No one is more familiar with the wild animals of Maine than Mr. Manly Hardy, the veteran woodsman and traveler of Brewer, Maine. We have no authentic information as to the occurrence of the panther in Maine — though newspaper tales of its presence abound — and application to Mr. Hardy draws from him the following characteristic note:

In answer to whether the panther (*Felis concolor*), more commonly called *catamount*, occurs in Maine, I will say that though my father and myself were buyers of fur for more than seventy-five years, neither of us ever saw the skin of one of these animals taken either in Maine, New Brunswick, Nova Scotia or Canada East. I have handled nearly or quite half a million dollars' worth of fur taken in the above places, but have yet to hear of a single skin being taken. The same is true of the wolverene or *carcarjou*, commonly called *Indian devil*, or *lunksoos*.

I have read scores of stories of both being taken, but unfortunately, they either have no skins or else they get lost on their way to market. It is but fair to say that I have had several reliable hunters tell me of seeing tracks of what they believed to be *catamounts*, and one who is well acquainted with animals has told me of wounding what he supposed to be one, but up to date I have never known of any positive proof of the animal ever being in Maine.

I have had dozens of men minutely describe *catamounts* they had seen, but from their descriptions I feel sure that what they saw were either Canada lynx or wildcats. It has been for many years a common thing in lumber and hunting camps to try to frighten tenderfeet with terrible stories of *catamounts, ding-mauls, side-winders* and other ferocious animals they were likely to meet. I remember in the spring of 1861 that as I traveled on foot over a hundred miles from Katahdin Iron Works to the headwaters of the St. John, I met many crews coming out who usually had frightful stories to tell me of the walruses and the danger I ran of meeting them. While it is possible there may have been *catamounts* in Maine, I should judge that the chances of meeting a walrus in our woods was about as great as seeing one of them.

— Manly Hardy

An additional response to the article by a Mr. William Wells provides additional details on the similarity and differences of panther and lynx tracks:

In the article "No Panthers in Maine" mention is made of panther tracks having been seen. The track of *Felis concolor* is in size and shape almost an exact counterpart of that of the Canada lynx. It often requires close scrutiny to distinguish the track of a big lynx from that of a panther. The stride is nearly the same, and owing to the fact that the ball and toes of the foot of the lynx are completely covered with fur, thus increasing the size, and the spread of the toes great, the footprints in snow are much alike.

The main difference is that the impression of the toes and ball of the foot in the lynx track are blurred and indistinct, owing to the fur, and the heel mark runs more to a point, while the footprint of the panther is clear cut and perfect, the heel mark being broad. Neither track will show any claw marks on level ground.

The big timber wolf has a track much like a panther, but the two middle toes project further ahead, making the footprint pointed instead of round, and the claw marks show.

— Wm. Wells

Panther in Maine
(Editor's Collection)

Taken 2021 at the Maine Wildlife Park, Gray Maine. The sign at the exhibit notes the last panther shot in Maine was in 1938, near the Quebec border. That would have been nearly thirty years after Manly Hardy's passing.

XV — On Sebec Lake

by
Anna Boynton Averill

At dusk we drifted out of Wilson stream,
Before the stars came, while the tender sky
Still wrapped the Borestone in a rosy dream,
And night drew near to see the sweet day die.

The low shore-hills loomed solemn, dark, and green,
Above the waters where their bases rest;
But all the farther, dimmer peaks were seen,
In fading mists of rose and purple dressed.

Slow drifting southward toward the summer night,
And the home hills uplifted far away,
Out of the sunset and the golden light
We went, among the twilight shadows gray.

From out the coolness of the wooded shore,
Sweet wafts of fir and fern and birch were blown;
And one bird's song repeated o'er and o'er
Followed our floating till the light had flown.

Then fireflies flashed among the thickets dark,
And stars came out above us and below;
* * * Oh, little boat wast thou a fairy bark
Between the earth and heaven drifting slow?

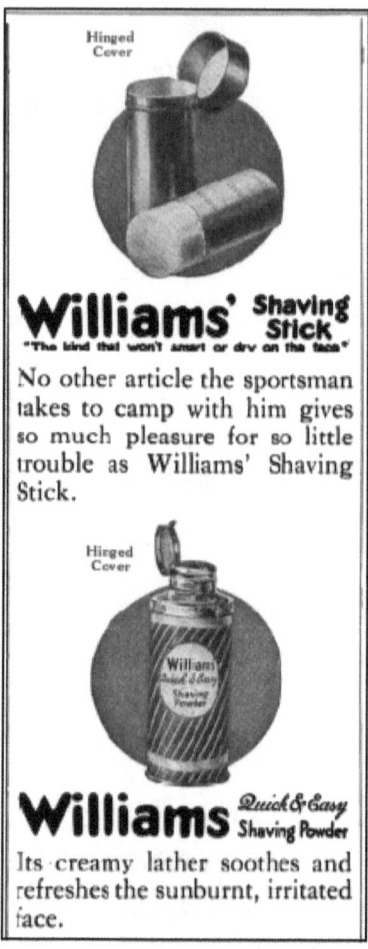

1890s Advertisement.

XVI — The Otters of Machias

Manly Hardy's final article in *Forest and Stream* is introduced by his daughter, Fannie Hardy Eckstorm. The reader is reminded that this article was written in a different age for a magazine where the main focus was hunting, fishing, and the outdoors. Manly Hardy was a woodsman who made his living by fur trading. His purpose here was to document, in the Hardy way, with facts on how things were.

For the last time, the name of Manly Hardy appears in *Forest and Stream*. This article on the otter was finished but thirty hours before he died, and less than an hour before he was made to take to his bed. He left nothing else prepared, no notes, and no journals from which anyone but himself could have worked. These are his ultimate words.

Begun when he was in his usual health and worked upon leisurely, a few pages at a time, it was finished under sharp pain and with the full anticipation of death coming soon. Yet no one but myself could tell at what point in it he decided that he was doing his last work and made haste to finish it. Up to the last word, it is the otter that he is hunting, and his only care is to leave some trustworthy information about its habits.

The night before he died I was with him, waiting upon him, and among other directions which he gave me was the instruction to go to his desk, where I would find the concluding pages of this sketch. He had not wanted to leave it unfinished, and he worked upon it up to the last moment. He had left off where he did, he said, wishing to consult me as to whether to add something about the great extinct mink and otter of the Maine coast, which he believed to be different species. I considered his own condition, and advised him that he had already once, some time ago, given *Forest and Stream* an article upon the seashore mink and otter, which seemed to be sufficient.

"Except for that, is it done?" I asked.

"Yes, all done. When you typewrite it, make any changes you wish to and send it in as my last contribution to *Forest and Stream*."

Here it is as he wrote, save only the minor changes always required in reducing hasty manuscript to a printable form. Those who would understand my father may read here the way in which he always faced death and danger, and will better understand that to those who knew him it was the omissions in his tales of personal adventure that were often the most significant parts of his relation.

> "Let others frame their creeds — mine is to work;
> To do my best, however far it fall
> Below the keener craft of stronger hands;
> To be myself, full-hearted, free and true
> To what my own soul sees, below, above;
> To think my own thought straight out from the heart;
> To feel and be, and never stop to ask:
> 'Do all men so? Is this the world's highway?'
> To look unflinching in the face of life
> As eagles look upon the noon-day sun;
> To cut my own path through primeval woods;
> To lay my own course by the polar star
> Across the trackless plains and mountains vast;

To seek, not follow, ever till the end.
And for the rest — bare-handed have I come
Into this world, I know not whence nor why.
Bare-handed and alone and unafraid,
With heart of fire and eyes that question still,
Will I go forth into the wide Beyond,
As went the men who bore my blood of old
To Eblis or Valhalla nothing loath."[65]

— F. H. E.

"The Otter"

by Manly Hardy
Forest and Stream
March 4, 1911, Vol. 76, No. 9 & 10.

One of our most interesting animals, and one concerning which very little reliable information can be found in books, is the otter. While otter are found in most parts of the United States and Canada, they vary very little in size, though those from the west coast average a little larger than those from New England and Canada. Otter from Maine and the Provinces are from four to four and one-half feet in length and usually weigh from eighteen to twenty pounds, twenty-five pounds being an exceptionally heavy weight.

While not gregarious in the sense of collecting in large numbers, still I know of no other of our fur-bearing animals,

---

[65] This poem was also at the beginning of Eckstorm's 1907 book, *David Libbey: Penobscot Woodman and River-driver.* (see Burnt Jacket Publishing Annotated Edition for further discussion on origin.)

except the beaver, which is so seldom seen solitary, and no other, not excepting squirrels, which spend so much time playing together. Two or three are seen together as commonly as one is seen alone. Often four or five are seen in company, and I have known of seven. When swimming, one is usually in the lead and the others follow in his wake with short intervals between each, and when their backs roll out of water as they swim, three or four will often look like one body thirty or forty feet in length. The seeing of several swimming in this manner has undoubtedly given rise to the stories often repeated in our newspapers of large fresh-water snakes being seen in our lakes. Usually if the one in the lead sees or smells anything suspicious, he will raise his head and neck, a foot or two above the water, looking very much as the head of a large snake would look, and as the others dive when he does, people not used to otter are not to blame for thinking they have seen an immense snake. This belief is further strengthened by seeing places in flag beds or on marshy points where it looks as if heavy bodies had been dragged. These places are made by the otters sliding over them.

There is one habit which many writers mention. This is the sliding for amusement. This otters indulge in at all seasons and in many different situations. Sometimes in winter when there is a little snow on the crust, they slide for rods on the crust where the land is nearly level. At other times, in summer and fall, they slide down banks only two or three feet above the water, or sometimes where the bank slopes for twenty to thirty feet, or sometimes in winter down banks of snow, and I have once seen where they slid down a bank of pure white sand which the spring freshet had heaped up ten or twelve feet high. In sliding they throw their forefeet back over their shoulders

and slide on their breasts. Whether they ever use their hind feet
to propel themselves in any cases is more than I can be positive
of; but I once followed two of them more than two miles across
a nearly flat bog and they slid fully half the way. There was a
light snow on the crust, but I could not see any evidence of
their using their hind feet when sliding. They will often slide
on a flag bed[66] where the water is only a few inches deep. I
have watched two otters slide across a flag bed ten or twelve
feet wide, one coming out of the water about the time that the
other went under, and repeating this scores of times, going so
swiftly that it looked as if an endless chain of otters was being
hauled across it.

While most animals occasionally quarrel with each other, I
have never heard of otters being seen fighting together, and in
handling some thousands of their skins I have never seen any
evidence of their biting one another. I have seen two mink,
which are a near relative to the otter, fighting like bulldogs,
and our snow-shoe rabbits often fight like cats, but if otters
ever quarrel with each other it must be very seldom. This is
not because they are not willing to fight with other animals or
with men, as I have known of several men being badly bitten
by them. Sometimes when attacked they give a sharp scream,
somewhat like the scream of a mink, only much louder. This
and a noise they make when they are calling each other are the
only noises I have ever heard of their making, except that I
have heard of one snoring when asleep, and when one rises out
of the water and smells a person he will snort or blow very
much as a seal does. In fact, in many ways they resemble seals,

---

[66] Flag bed is term for flowery growth, in this case, maybe moose-
ear.

especially in the way they will rise up straight in the water with head and neck exposed, and in the way they rise with a fish in the mouth.

Otters will sometimes whip a large dog in a fair fight. I know of one case where there was a large bulldog with a lumber crew. The landing sawyers heard him all the afternoon barking down near the outlet of the pond, and as he did not come to camp at night, they went in search of him with a lantern. They found him lying between a dead otter and the otter's hole. He had killed the otter, but was himself too badly hurt to move. Some writers state that "no dog ever killed an otter in a fair fight." This is an error, as there are many dogs that can do it. Once my father when hunting moose found the tracks of three otters which were crossing over high land in making a short cut from one pond to another. His companion had with him a quite small dog which had been trained to kill animals in traps by backing up to them and letting them jump on his back, when he would wheel and catch them by the throat. In this case on coming to the otter, the one he attacked rose on his hind feet and jumped on the dog's back. The first two times the dog got the otter by the throat he was thrown several feet to one side, but the third time he held his grip and did not let go until the otter was dead. The dog did not get hurt. This I know, as I well remember helping an Indian skin the otter.[67]

---

[67] The reason for his remembering so well was that a horse, scared by the smell of otter grease which the Indian had playfully rubbed on him, kicked my father in the temple and nearly killed him outright. — F. H. E

In another case my old friend William H. Staples was crossing some burned land when there was snow and came upon the tracks of three otters. He had with him a large bulldog which took the track, and when Staples came up, the dog had one of the otters dead. I came into the Seboois House only a few minutes after Staples came in with the skin. The dog showed no signs of being bitten. If there was any fight it must have been a very short one, as the first Staples knew of it was finding the dog with the dead otter. I think any dog which can kill a large raccoon can kill an otter if he can have the otter on the land. Certainly, such dogs as they have in the West trained to fight mountain lions and coyotes, would make short work of an otter, as although very tough and good fighters, no animal not weighing over twenty-five pounds and having little help from claws can be a match for a large dog trained to fight wild animals.

In one case I know of three otters making common cause and beating a man. Two men, with both of whom I was well acquainted, were deer hunting and were traveling parallel with each other and not far apart. One of them, called Crooked-eyed Joe Penney, came upon three otters and fired at and wounded one. The otter fell, and Penney, who had a single-shot muzzleloader, rushed up to get him when the others attacked him. He broke the stock of his rifle and bent the barrel in trying to kill them, with the result that he was badly bitten and his trousers nearly torn off, while the otters, including the wounded one, escaped. Penney told me that he bent his rifle in pounding their heads and that he might as well have pounded a bag of wool as far as hurting them; but the opinion of his partner and myself was that he was so excited that he struck over and bent his rifle by striking the ground, as I have known of otter being killed by a few blows from a scale rule,[68] a goad stick or a pitch-fork handle, and in several instances I have known them killed where the man had nothing but his feet and hands. The well-known guide, T. W. Billings, of Brownville, Me., once told me that one time he was crossing a bog to look at an otter trap, when he met an old otter and two young ones. He tried to kill one of the young ones by jumping on it when the old one attacked him and, as he said, made him take steps that a dancing master would never have taught him. He finally killed one of the young ones, but was badly bitten.

There are few animals as quick as an otter. When looking at a person they will dodge a bullet as quickly as a seal can. I once fired at one which had his head out of his fishing hole in the ice. The ball struck not six inches beyond in the exact range of the center of the hole, but the otter had drawn his head down before it struck. I have known of many cases where they dived before the charge struck. They will catch any fish we have by chasing it as a cat chases a mouse. A friend of mine while fishing in a pool just below a small fall, saw several large trout come rushing over the fall, and almost at the same time he saw something which, as he said, looked like a shadow, pursuing them round the pool, and an instant after an otter raised his head with one of the trout in his mouth.

While they feed on trout where trout are plentiful, otters also eat all kinds of coarser fish — chubs, suckers and horned pouts. I have several times seen them eating eels, which they

---

[68] A scale rule is used to estimate the amount of lumber, in board feet, that will be cut from a log. An excellent reference on lumbering is, *"Tall Trees, Tough Men,"* by Robert E. Pike, W. W. Norton & Co., (1967).

seem to prefer to anything else. Sometimes when fish are plentiful and easy to catch, the otter will kill them for sport, just as too many of our visiting fishermen do. I have known one to pile up a large lot of suckers which he had caught for the fun of it. Besides fish, they often catch muskrats, and in winter I have known them to entirely depopulate the houses of a large colony of muskrats. When in a beaver country they often kill the young beaver, and I feel quite sure that they also sometimes kill ducks. I was once being paddled up to a black duck which we had heard quacking in a logan;[69] I saw what I thought were the backs of several ducks and beyond them just then a duck gave a loud quack and flew. I then saw that what I had taken for ducks were two otters which seemed to be trying to catch the furthest duck. While they were underwater, I put a charge of BBs in one barrel, and on their rising with their heads close together, I killed one and wounded the other. The same fall the man who was paddling me on this occasion saw two otters trying to catch some wood ducks.

Otters are very tenacious of life and often escape when shot squarely through the body and sometimes when shot through the head, especially when on the ice. An Indian named Louis Nicholas crept close to one's fishing hole while the otter was under water. The otter came out with a trout in his mouth and lay on the ice facing the Indian. The trout being before his eyes hindered him from seeing the Indian, who fired a Spencer rifle ball which went into the mouth and out through the back of the

---

[69] The Indian word *pokelogan* was interpreted by Thoreau as an inlet that led nowhere. *Logan* is a shortened form and means a shallow place. Lumbermen would speak of 'loganning' logs, when they stored them in logans (source: Eckstorm).

otter's head, carrying brains out on the ice, but the otter dived into his hole and the Indian and his partner, after cutting ice and looking for him nearly half a day, were unable to find him. The partner told me that both brains and teeth lay on the ice when he went to help search for the otter.

I once bought of an Indian the skin of an otter which had an ounce ball fairly through the body just back of the shoulders. This otter, which was shot lying on the ice, dived into his hole, and after being under a long time. suddenly threw himself out of another hole some rods from the one he entered and died almost as soon as he struck the ice. I have known many times of otter fairly shot being lost, and on the other hand, several times of two being killed at a shot and both saved, and in one case of three shot and all secured. A hunting partner of mine once killed and got three otters at two shots from a rifle in less than a minute's time. I once bought the skins of four otters, all shot in one forenoon by one man.

I have known of several otters being got in singular ways. Rufus B. Philbrook,[70] who had been my partner the year before, was traveling on snowshoes up the Allagash Stream above the lake. On turning a bend in the stream, he saw an otter lying on the ice and fired at him with his ten-inch rifled pistol. As the otter lay still he supposed that he had killed him, but seeing his eye look bright as he came up, he struck the otter with his belt hatchet. On skinning him, Philbrook found that the otter had not been touched by the bullet. In another instance a man who was not hunting, but who carried a

---

[70] For more on Rufus Philbrook, see, *Exploring the Maine Woods – The Hardy Family Expedition to the Machias Lakes*, Burnt Jacket Publishing, (2021).

revolver, came to a place where otters had been playing in the light snow around some fishing holes. Seeing a patch of dark fur showing through the snow, he fired and found that he had shot a dead otter. It appeared as if the otter had died on the ice and then it had snowed on him, and the other otter in playing had partly uncovered him.

When otters are caught in log slide-traps, or killheags, other otters quite often cover them up nicely with moss or leaves. I have several times seen where mink had so covered other mink which were in log traps, but have never heard of either mink or otters doing it to an animal which was in a steel trap. When otters are trapped where they cannot get into the water, they will fight a trap terribly, and if they cannot pull out or break the chain, will usually kill themselves in a short time. No one who has not seen it would believe how an otter can twist the links of a chain which has no swivel in it. I have seen a chain which seemed strong enough to hold a horse broken by an otter. I have twice set traps on Saturday afternoon and on Monday forenoon have found otter dead from fighting the trap, which appeared to have been dead for twenty-four hours. When caught on the land they usually break most of their teeth in fighting the trap, and I have several times seen the whole end of the lower jaw broken, and I have had several of the old-fashioned hand-made traps which plainly showed the marks of otter's teeth on the bedpieces.

Usually otters have but two young, but I have known of their having three. Some writers speak of more, but I very much doubt their having more than three.

Otters seldom stay more than a few days in one place no matter how plentiful the fish are. The Indians say: "Otter don't happy in Heaven." A family will have a route which they will follow as regularly as a Methodist circuit rider. Sometimes it will be only fifteen or twenty miles, but oftener twice as much, which round they will make in from two to four weeks, going through chains of ponds, up or down streams and sometimes making carries on land for quite long distances, sometimes meeting others, but oftener one party coming into a pond soon after another has left. When one sees tracks of otters leaving the water and going overland, he may be sure that they are taking the shortest route to some other water.

In winter otters make fishing holes through quite thick ice just as seals do. As their noses are formed so as to shut air-tight they can swim across large ponds under the ice just as beaver or muskrats do, by putting their noses against the ice and throwing out a bubble, which looks like that in a spirit level, and renewing their breath by drawing it in again. If not disturbed they can swim any distance in this way; but if driven away from their air-bubble, they soon drown.

In places where the snow drifts deep over the banks on the edges of streams or ponds, they often have places under the snow banks where they bring out their fish and eat them.

Often the fur of otters taken in the winter has the long outer hairs curled or kinked at the end like card teeth. This is called "sun curl" by the fur buyers and is supposed to be caused by the reflection of the sun from the ice. Yet this hardly seems a satisfactory explanation as I have seen them as badly curled early in December as at any time late in the winter; but I have never seen one taken after the ice was out that was so curled.

How deep an otter dives when fishing no one knows, but I know positively of two cases where otters were taken on lines set for togue with live bait in deep water. One was on Moosehead Lake, the other in one of the Roach River Ponds, probably in not less than twenty feet of water. In these cases, the otters got hooked in catching the live bait, just as the togue would have done, and as the line was fastened to a spring pole which would bend, and as he could not get his feet on bottom, he drowned much quicker than a fish would have drowned.

I once knew of a man, who was pulling a pickerel through a hole in the ice, feeling a suddenly increased resistance which continued until he hauled the head of an otter into sight. The otter had seized the pickerel as it was being drawn up and had held on until he saw the man, when he bit the fish in two and left the fisherman in possession of the head part. Sometimes large fish escape from otters, and I once saw a large pickerel whose back was deformed, evidently from having been bitten by an otter, as the scar was plainly to be seen on both sides.

While in handling over half a million of muskrats, I have seen but a single albino, yet in handling not over a hundredth part as many otters I have seen five pure white ones and another of a yellowish white. As these were all taken within a few years in quite a limited area, it seemed as if the albinism were transmitted, especially as R. McFarlane, the Hudson Bay factor, while he speaks of sometimes seeing white beaver and some other kinds, does not mention ever seeing an albino otter. It is a singular thing, that of the five pure white ones that I know, three were shot. I saw two of them before they were skinned. The fourth was said to have been caught by a man in his hands as the otter was diving into a hole in the ice; he was held till he drowned. I had the skin of this one. It was a very large skin and as white as "the driven snow" and showed no mark of either trap or bullet. I do not know how the fifth was taken, but it seemed singular that when not one otter in twenty is taken except in traps, that four out of five white ones should not have been trapped. I know of one other white otter being taken near where these were. Besides these, I have in over sixty years never heard of but three others being taken, one in New Brunswick and bought by C. & E. Everett, King's Square, St. John, N. B., and the others taken in Maine, one at Blue Hill and the other in the western part of the State.

— Manly Hardy

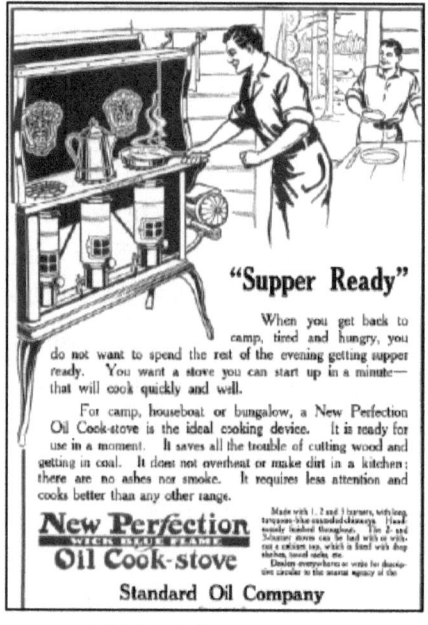

1890s Advertisement

XVII — A Bird Song

by
Anna Boynton Averill

O, summer bird, the soft wind shakes
    The light leaf shadows o'er thy breast!
Thy quivering throat is full of song
    That with the wind doth rock thy nest!

This dell, a dimple in the wood,
    Is wild and sweet enough for thee;
    — I sit alone and listen long,
    For O, thy song doth comfort me!

It falleth sweeter than the rain
    That dropping cool on thirsty leaves,
Doth wash them clear of every stain
    The hot and dusty weather weaves —

    — Shy spirit! while thou singest here,
    All careless of my love — or me,
I hold thee in my heart most dear,
    And draw divine content from thee.

A Downy Woodpecker
(Editor's Collection)

XVIII — A Question Of Taste

Forest and Stream – November 14, 1889

FOR many months in the year the two mountain ash or "roundwood" trees under my windows are a favorite place of resort for birds of all kinds: but of the many interesting observations which these trees have offered me, the most interesting relates to a question of taste, raised by the birds. A fool may ask questions, they say, but it takes a wise man to answer them; and the birds, though no fools, have not usurped the wise man's province, so that at best the question must wait for its answer.

In brief, there is a difference between these trees. They are both large for their kind, of equal age, similarly situated, to all appearances precisely alike, except that the one on the right sheds its leaves before the other, and is an inch or two less in girth. There seems nothing to choose between them, yet the birds know a difference, which I, not having a nice taste in roundwood berries, could never detect. That connoisseur of small fruits, the robin, will sit all day on one of them and eat roundwood berries till you wonder how his tonnage is rated, with what

> "Particular addition from the bill
> Which writes them all alike."

But not a berry of the other tree will he touch. As the robin's taste always agrees exactly with mine in the selection of strawberries, cherries and currants, he invariably securing the ones I intended to have — (It is a mistake to say that the early bird gets the worm; he leaves that for you) — I would unhesitatingly assert that if there is anything good in the line of roundwood berries he knows it and has his share of it. In the winter the pine grosbeaks visit these trees in large flocks, and although they eat the seed only, rejecting the pulp, they confirm the robins' decision that the tree on the left is a superior article. In the spring, if the yield has been abundant and the grosbeaks few, the purple finches finish the work of stripping the trees, and by these also the tree on the left is preferred; while there is a single berry on it the birds flock to it to the neglect of the other, which may be hanging with almost unbroken clusters; yet when there is nothing more left on the favorite tree, they resort to the other and find food, if not epicurean satisfaction, in its full bunches of berries. For twenty years the same preference has been remarked, and the same agreement among all species of birds. De gustibus non disputandum, — *there's no accounting for tastes*, says the proverb, with a strong hint as to the reason; but in such a case as this, where the agreement cannot be doubted, while we may throw a sop to the proverb by allowing that a taste for roundwood berries is unaccountable on any grounds known to us, we must admit that this unanimity of opinion among the birds argues the existence of substantial grounds.

Granting this, what is the cause?

Whence has the fruit its flavor?

The birds asked the question and they must help answer it. "Let the sapsucker be called as the principal witness."

"May it please the Court, the sapsucker has a doubtful reputation. He is accused of irregular proceedings, and he bears a bad name. It is our point to show that he deserves his name. Until that is done his testimony will be worth little."

At the present day there is so little doubt of the yellow-bellied woodpecker's object in tapping trees, that even the naturalists have agreed, for the time being, to call him "the sapsucker." There are still some of those good people who, out of pure benevolence, would tell white lies to screen the devil, who aver that the yellow-bellied woodpecker eats nothing but worms; but if he should get a little sap now and then we ought not to grudge him that little. This is not the question whether the sapsucker is injurious or not. For my part, if he is content to draw a few ounces of sap from my trees while I drain them of gallons, he is welcome to all he gets, and to more, too. We do not wish to rob him of his good name as an eater of grubs and insects; we forbear to accuse him of any evil intent in tapping our trees; we wish to learn simply this — whether he gets anything besides worms (and bark, perhaps) out of those little holes which he places with such regularity around the branches of our fruit trees. Appearances are against him. For a bud that is ostensibly vermivorous, the sapsucker looks for his worms in such unsuitable places that he lays himself open to the same suspicion which attached to Sam Weller on that occasion in the court room, when the judge bade him report if he saw his father, and he, gazing steadfastly at the skylight, was able to answer in the negative with a good conscience.[71]

---

[71] Sam Weller, the character in *The Pickwick Papers* (1836), by Charles Dickens. In court, he is asked by the judge if he sees his own father. Sam looks up at the roof and answers, "No, I don't, my Lord."

I myself have watched the sapsucker frequently at his work. He comes with a headlong flight, alights with a sudden flap of his wings, as if he had been brought up unexpectedly by the tree when he thought he was steering past it; looks quickly around, like a person who has fallen on the ice, to see whether anyone saw his mishap, and soon addresses himself to his work. First, he taps the tree, sinking three or four rows of holes on the same or on different branches, and then he tends out on them, watching as lazily to see the sap flow into the holes, drinking out of each as it overflows, and sits thus half a day at a time, without moving three feet, enjoying the double satisfaction of anticipation and participation. If this is not proof enough, we have Mr. Maurice Thompson's statement that the sapsucker has been seen in the act of drinking sap from the farmers' sugar troughs.

It is not an assumption to claim that he loves sap "for sap's sake." Does he show any decided taste in sap, as the robin does in cherries, as the red headed woodpecker does in pears?

We know that the sapsucker prefers some species of trees to others, and some individual trees to others of the same species; and from the character of his holes we can judge very nearly whether he was after grubs or sap. If grubs were his principal object, of course he would not care what kind of sap the trees yielded; but if sap was what he wanted, may we not infer that his choice of trees would depend more or less on the taste of the sap?

Just here an obstacle confronts us. Tastes differ. In this region the sapsucker works chiefly on fruit trees, birches, swamp-maple shoots and young softwood trees — hemlock, firs and spruces — these, perhaps, for their soft inner bark. We favor the rock maple, which he seems not to affect. If we are judges of sweet sap only and he of other kinds, how can we reach an agreement? We know that there is a difference in the sap of the maple trees; some is better flavored, some renders a greater proportion of sugar; but where is the judge of apple sap?

Then again, our observations are insufficient. While it is well known that in an orchard some trees are much frequented by sapsuckers and others are left almost unscarred by them, I have never seen it anywhere stated that the sapsucker preferred either sour or sweet apple trees, or that they selected those which bear well-flavored fruit and rejected the crabbed; that is, that there is any sensible connection between the taste of the sap and the taste of the fruit.

It is still a question of taste, but how complicated. From the sapsucker's preference we infer a difference in flavor as the cause; but few of us know experimentally whether there is such a difference; most of us would be at a loss to detect it if we made the trial; we are unable to prove that it is the taste and not some other quality of sap which attracts him; lastly, we are met with the general question whether the taste of the sap is any index of the quality of the fruit or not.[72]

---

[72] A particular scientific study of the sapsucker tree feeding preference was conducted over one-hundred years after Eckstorm published this essay. The results were, "a coefficient of concordance test suggested that Yellow-bellied Sapsuckers do not select feeding tree species based on relative abundance." In other words, additional research was needed. [Reference: McLenon, L. Amanda, "Sap tree feeding preference by Yellow-bellied Sapsuckers (Sphyrapicus varius) based on tree size and

Let us interview the mountain ash trees again and learn what they have to say about the sapsucker.

There can be no doubt that he has been here. One tree is tattooed like the wild man from Borneo, from one end to the other, with little round holes set in horizontal lines, extending partly or wholly around the trunk and the branches. This is unmistakably "His Mark." Ten years will not suffice to outgrow this writing; twenty years is scarcely too long to do it in the mountain ash bark. Here stands the punctured record of many individuals and many years. Let us read it. One tree, we said, was covered with marks; the other is but little scarred. Twenty to one, at the lowest estimate, in favor of the tree on the left. You see the sapsuckers agree with the robins and other birds.

Here at last we get a little light on our questions. The sapsucker certainly does have a taste in sap. He has tried both trees; he chooses one. That he did not do it for anything but sap, or a little bark, repeated observations within 20 feet have demonstrated. We accepted without hesitation the robin's verdict on the berries of these trees. We know by experiment that his palate has the same gust as ours in all the articles of diet which we enjoy in common; and here we believed that our judgment would agree with his decision. Shall we refuse to believe what the sapsucker tells us, that there is a difference in

----

species in Cheboygan County, northern lower Michigan," August 1997, University of Michigan Biological Station.] Subsequently, additional research was published in 2015. The results indicated that "foraging   preference of sapsuckers differ significantly among tree species." Which is to say, the results were consistent with the simple Eckstorm observational method of 1889.

sap, and that he prefers one tree to the other solely on that account? Preference is a more limited term than judgment. We prefer maple sap to the neglect of all other kinds; but in giving our deliberate judgment on the respective products of these two roundwood trees, can there be much doubt that we should corroborate the decision of the sapsuckers and the robins?

One more query was raised, which we cannot undertake to answer, whether the taste of the sap sensibly conditions the taste of the fruit. The case of these mountain ash trees is remarkable enough to draw out the question, and their conditions are so exactly alike as far as can be determined, that it seems as if by the method of exclusion, the taste of the sap would be the only element left to account for the flavor of the fruit — as if one must be the cause of the other. But we cannot be too careful in determining causes. Extended experiment only can settle such a question, though a bird might raise it.

The roundwood trees have but one thing more to add, and this has been said before often enough, that the pricking's of the sapsuckers do not appear to be injurious. You may see for yourself that the trees he works on are apt to be the healthiest. As well say they are so, because of, as in spite of his interference; the professor would tell you that either way it is a *post hoc ergo propter hoc*, which is only another warning to be careful about assigning causes.[73]

— Fannie Pearson Hardy

---

[73] Students of statistics will surely remember that *correlation, does not suggest causality.*

Eckstorm's observations on birds extended to publishing the books, *The Woodpeckers* (1901) and *The Bird Book* (1901), which became references for ornithologists and casual bird observers alike.

XIX — The White Throated Sparrow

by
Anna Boynton Averill

Far away a wood bird sings
　In the spruce's purple shade,
And I follow at the call
　Down a leafy cool arcade.
O, how far, how clear, how pure,
　Is this liquid floating song!
Sweet bird spirit! Vain my quest
　Though I hear you all day long,
　　　"Come, come, follow me, follow me."

Here a sparrow builds her home
　In the creviced, mossy ledge,
And a startled redwing flies
　Like a fire spark from the hedge.
And the dusky wood is filled
　With clear songs and flitting wings
While I follow wrapped in dreams
　Where this lonely spirit sings
　　　"Come, come, follow me, follow me."

And I hope that some white day
   In the cool wood shadows deep,
I shall end my patient search
   And a rich reward shall reap —
In the solemn mystic shade
   Where his dreamy music rings
I shall see my spirit bird.
   Hark! how sweet the song he sings,
      "Come, come, follow me, follow me."

White-Throated Sparrow
from, The Bird Book, Figure 56. (Eckstorm, 1901)

XX — Winter Fishing

Forest and Stream – November 28, 1889

ONCE upon a time a very learned professoress was met in the way by an Audubon committee.[74] With dejected looks the committee declared themselves unable by all their joint and several allurements to entrap any learned ornithologist into addressing their next Audubon meeting; ornithologists proved much too shy birds to be caught by any of their chaff, and had constitutional disinclinations to addressing Audubon societies. But, added the depressed committee, a certain justly celebrated entomologist who knew nothing at all about birds would be pleased to aid them in their difficulty.

"Ah!" said the learned professoress, looking very owl-like, "what is the connection between the two?"

The committee always gave up conundrums.

"I see," said the professoress, looking trebly wise, "birds eat insects. Let us invite the entomologist."

And he came.

If any ill-naturedly ask the connection between birds and *winter fishing*, be it known that birds eat fish as well as insects. Even in this region, where the mercury curls itself up in the bulb most of the winter, in order to keep itself warm, and the

---

[74] Fannie Pearson Hardy was the co-founder of the Smith College Audubon Chapter.

wind often blows furiously from the top of old Katahdin, while four months of unbroken sleighing is nothing unheard of, winter fishing ranks among sports. Far be it from us to say anything against an occupation which demands so much endurance and stout-heartedness. The man who has tried it will not speak lightly of the wind-burn and sun-burn, the snow-blind and the bitter cold of these great fallow lakes, miles in extent, plowed by the north wind until they lie welted with long, irregular ridges of snow and alternating furrows of flinty ice. A road across them is marked only by a line of bushes, set at intervals to guide the teamsters, and except this line of low, green bushes, nothing breaks the monotony of whiteness.

The lake in winter is one glittering level, whose length and breadth are indeterminable. It is whiteness unrelieved, without perspective, absorbing everything into itself, giving only an impression of blankness. The uncertainty of the judgment is increased rather than diminished by reference to the rim of the shore. The first impression of whiteness, the whiteness of molten metal if the sun is shining, is succeeded by one of loneliness. The open sea, the sandy desert, the barren plain, the lone and skyey mountain peak, do not give a greater idea of separateness from the world than do these lone, wintry lakes. Then there is the stillness — oppressive, horrible, obtruding itself into notice. It is a stillness like a magic spell. No wonder the owls living in such desolation go stark mad.

But the winter fisherman does not court the solitude of these great lakes. He bides under the shore — the lee shore, if a good fishing ground happens to be on that side — where he can hear sounds more companionable than the hollow bellowing of the ice. There is always an awfulness about these heavy groans and mugient reverberations heard at a distance, and swelling in crescendo as they pass under foot, to which one never can become indifferent. These muffled noises speak to our credulity of an unknown about us. It is the voice of the blinded Polyphemus roaring in his rocky cavern that he is the victim of Woman.[75] Even the noise of trees cracked by the frost or beaten by the wind is preferable to these unearthly and unaccountable sounds.

Polyphemus as the *Victim of Woman*

Following this essay installment in Forest and Stream, Hardy (Eckstorm) provided the following addendum to her article in the next issue.

We are willing to forgive the compositor much — misspellings, abbreviations which we never thought of writing, and a free and easy style of punctuation which puts most of the work on the commas; we will bear in meekness all reasonable objurgations on the subject of poor penmanship; we will even forbear to scold the editor if matters are not borne according to our mind; infallibility is as far from us as from the compositor. But is it not a little too much to be made to say that Polyphemus was "the victim of Woman?" We protest against the use of our name in any such libel on a sex of which we are justly proud, and of which we would say no harm, whatever the room for improvement.

---

[75] This is an original Forest and Stream editor mis-correction that was too wonderful not to leave. See the inset.

The allusion was to Odysseus's visit to the Cyclops, to whom he gives an assumed name:

"Cyclops, thou hast asked me my illustrious name,
No-man is my name, and No-man father, mother and
All my comrades call me."— (Odyssey IX)

Later, when Odysseus has blinded the Cyclops, the wounded giant calls out to his fellows:

"No-man is slaying me by craft and not by force,"

who, understanding him to say that *no one* is troubling him either by craft or by force, reply:

"If no one harms thee, and thou art alone,
Reflect there is no way to escape great Jove;
But pray thou to thy father Neptune."

But the joke — one of the grimmest in literature — acquires a new and heightened horror by making poor, unoffending Woman the giant killer.
— Brewer, Me. Fannie Pearson Hardy.

As to the reason the printer/editor changed, what Eckstorm correctly wrote as "no one," to "woman," that is a mystery of "typesetting." I find it wonderful how she took such a tactful method to correct the printer. I wonder if the printer read and understood her fanciful errata. I have been reminded of more than the mythology of "no one" today.

After the fisherman has cut his holes through the thick, clear ice, and put in his "gang" of lines, fastening them to limber "spring poles" or to ingenious "tip-ups," which are intended to give notice when any fish bites the hook, he is free to build himself a fire under the shore, perhaps against some granite boulder, shaggy with tough black lichen, which, pursuant to the providence that cares for the shorn lamb by giving him a new suit of clothes, while it leaves the wind to the charge of the Weather Bureau, covers these exposed rocks with a garment like leather, as if to atone for the inclemencies of then-position. All along the shores of our lakes and on the brows of our mountains, wherever the granite crops out, it is sure to be ornamented with these rosettes, brown on the outer surface and black beneath, and as dry as if grown expressly for a *hortus siccus*.[76] A fire on ice is certainly good for little unless for its company and the work needed to take care of it. You cannot warm yourself by it; you cannot dry your mittens by it, except with great odds on the side of getting them burned; you can have no comfort near it, for on whatever side of it you place yourself it will puff smoke into your eyes; but the red flames are a pleasant reminder of warmth, and the smoke, rising and drifting away to leeward, often toles a few small birds to the spot where they may find company, for the smaller kinds are creature-loving things.

Most of the day is passed on the ice in tramping from one fish-hole to another, bailing out the slush and fast-forming ice, rebaiting the hooks, and keeping sharp watch on the spring poles. What little there is to see tends rather to strain the eyes

---

[76] Hortus siccus, an arranged collection of dried plants.

than to rest them. The slender spring poles, some of them so far away as to look of scarcely more than a hair's breadth — such wands as Robin Hood never shot at — so slight that being gazed at intently, they seem to bend when they do not bend; the narrow track of a fox stretching away across the lake until it is lost in the level whiteness, yet continually tempting the eyes to trace it a little further; a dark object on the ice which may be large, may be small, far or near, but which at all events must be visited before its size can be known; the wide expanse of dazzling snow, itself as undetermined as everything upon it; all these things weary the brain far more than they do the eyes.

Even the sky affords little relief. It is as measureless as the lake itself. Few of our city dwellers know the wonderful clearness of our northern winter skies, which in purity of color rival the summer skies, and in delicacy of tint surpass them. In bright weather, for days at a time, there will be scarcely a cloud across the blue, until the sunset paints clouds where we had seen none. Before an approaching storm they often assume royal hues — green, blue and purple, colors whose depth and splendor are neither seen nor appreciated by inhabitants of smoky towns.

In such a dearth of sights and sounds our eyes and ears, both accustomed to being overcharged and capable of disentangling hardly more than a centesimal of the impressions which besiege them constantly, now suffer as if in a vacuum. Instead of selecting, merely they are compelled to change their habit and actually to seek for sensations. Every little sound suddenly acquires value. The chirring of a squirrel, the rattle of a logcock[77] hammering a green hemlock,[78] the sharp cry of a hairy woodpecker, the lisp of redpolls flying over, become suddenly prominent. There is a most welcome break in this unnatural stillness, which makes all sounds seem distant, and the ears hypersensitive, when, after a time, the red-bellied nuthatches and chickadees smelling the smoke, follow it up and flit about confiding and curious, frequently making work for themselves in order the better to watch the fisherman's movements. Sometimes also those gray-headed miscreants, the meat-birds,[79] come whistling about, and succeed before the visit is over in lugging off an assortment of things they do not want, chuckling over their knavery. There is no hope for the meat-bird — none; he is incorrigible.

The chickadees are the greatest favorites of all, however, and the most social and trustful. I shall always remember some which visited my father and myself five years ago. It was one of the worst days of the winter — clear and bright, but bitterly cold, and with a keen north wind which drove through our heavy robes as if they had been burlaps. Eight miles from

---

[77] "Logcock" is the hunter's name for the pileated woodpecker, *Ceophloeus pileatus* Cab. (Linn.). (Ref. original)

[78] In the September 1902 edition of Birds and Nature (Vol. 12, No. 4), Manly Hardy is quoted with, "The Pileated Woodpecker is a constant resident of Maine, but rarely leaves the vicinity of large timber. It prefers places where large hemlocks abound, especially those localities where a few have been killed by camp building or small fires."

[79] "Meatbird" is a common Maine name for the "Whisky Jack" or Canada jay, Perisoreus canadensis Bonap. (Linn.). (Ref. original)

home prudence counseled us to return; ten miles away and pride would have yielded, *"if it hadn't come so far already."* We got all the lee there was and built a fire; but there was little comfort in it. At noon our bait pail made ice, although it stood full in the sun, and within three feet of a good fire. At dinner time we partially thawed our frozen food, and made some coffee to hasten the thawing process a little. As we ate, some hungry little chickadees that had been digging for wood worms came up to us, probably attracted by the smell of food. They lighted on the robes, looking up confidently with their big heads cocked on one side, as if to say, "You don't care, now, do you?" and helped themselves.

What a dinner we had!

Two of us entertaining four chickadees and proud of the honor. They ate everything — meat, bread, mince pie, orange even. We tried them to see if they would pick at the orange peel, but although they were attracted by the color, they never mistook it for the pulp. Fortunately, these winter birds like salted food, so the chickadees fared well. They grew more and more familial. They brushed our faces with their wings as they flitted past. One lighted in my greasy tin plate and slipped about in it unable to get any footing, looking up meanwhile with the drollest possible air, which said, "Quite a rink, quite a rink, for a small chap like me."

Another actually alighted on my hand, and sitting on my forefinger ate meat which I fed to him. Could anyone ever forget the thrill those tiny, clasping bird's claws gave? We came home happy.

Fish? Yes, one about the size of a clothespin; but we didn't go for fish that day.

The only other authentic instance that I have of equal tameness of any wild bird was reported last winter by a woodchopper. He said that several chickadees stayed about his chopping for a long time, ate his luncheon with him, frequently lighted on his person, and one even allowed him to stroke it with his finger as it sat on a bush.

Ostensibly the winter fisherman goes for fish. In reality, whoever believed that a string of slimy, broad-snouted pickerel paid him for his work and exposure and suffering? No matter if their mottled hides outshone the jaguar's and their bellies were overlaid with silver, they would not be worth the trouble. They serve only as an excuse, and their attraction does not compare with the strength of that savage desire to taste solitude, and for the space of a day to feel the loneliness of barbarism.

— Fannie Pearson Hardy

Pileated Woodpecker
(Editor's Collection)

A Frozen Maine Lake
(Editor's Collection)

XXI — The Brook

Forest and Stream – December 12, 1889

THERE is a brook — a tiny little brook, so small that it might properly be called a brooklet — which trickles down through a hillside orchard so old and mossy and shagbarked that it can scarcely tell itself from the pine grove on the knoll above, and drops musically (the brook now, not the orchard) over stones not thicker than your hand, gurgling with a diminutive murmur suited to its own diminutive size, around clean pebbles, spreading out over sandy shallows as large as your palm, or maybe larger where they are very large, and losing itself in a great forest of forget-me-nots a rod square, until after a quarter-mile of such wandering it gets down to the pond where the great bullfrog lives. It is strange if you never heard of this brook; for a poet lives right beside it, a lady whom you all know, and a novelist, a very famous novelist, whom you all know, too, lives just beyond, and nearby a professor whom you all ought to know; but I am not aware that the poet or the novelist or the professor care very much for the little brook, which is left to babble on to its ferns and apple trees and its pines and forget-me-nots.

However, the birds know it, all of them, and trim little sparrows delight to flirt in and out of brush piles on the bank, playing hide-and-go-seek with themselves; warblers beyond number inspect the old apple tree boughs every morning, and great fat robins take the whole stream to bathe in, covering both banks with their motherly wings. There is no danger of the birds forgetting the little brooklet. All winter long in the far South they think of it, and it is the first place they visit in the spring, passing by the pond where the great bullfrog says *per-r-uke* and the middle-sized frogs say *tr-r-ronk*, and the little ones (which the learned professor declares are not frogs at all, but toads), being neither wig dealers nor trunk makers, keep up an auction din by proclaiming that their articles are *cheap! cheap!* In the spring the birds fly directly past this Vanity Fair and seek the brooklet cuddled down among the apple trees and pines.

If anyone has a mind to wait here, lying at the foot of the big white pine on a bed of brown pine needles, with curtains of low bushes and the sky for a tester — if anyone has a mind to lie here all the morning, and can forget that he belongs to a very busy world which is moiling and toiling and hammering its life out half a mile away, he may see wonders. For the little birds, after they have splashed and drunk, and drunk and splashed, to their hearts' content, grow very tame and come close up to him, so close that he can see their bright little eyes, the bristles about their tiny bills and their sharp little toenails.

Somehow everything about the brooklet is little, just as it should be; and if anyone lies down beside it for a time, and doesn't think too hard, he will find himself shrinking, small, smaller, until at last he is about as large as a happy, well-fed baby, and there is no mistake about this, though the professor didn't tell it to me.

This may be the reason why the birds are so tame, but whether it is or isn't, they will come to you as you lie there, just as I have told you, a long procession of them. First there is the robin; but he doesn't come very near, for he knows all about you, has seen you downtown many the times, and you can't tell him anything. So after his bath the robin sits on the fence-post and tries to make you believe that the welfare of the world depends on his being in that particular place. But the song thrush and the veery who have not moved in society as much as the robin, show their country breeding by their curiosity, and come and perch on the dry pine limb nearby, quite shy and silent unless the veery gives a tender little serenade that seems to come from far, far away. By and by, when you least expect it, there is a soft flutter of brown wings and the large-eyed visitors are off.

Hardly have the thrushes gone before an inquisitive black and yellow warbler, in all the bravery of his new spring coat, lights on the swaying limb and eyes you with as much self-possession as if you were the intruder, not he — a gay fellow with his striped waistcoat of black and yellow, a regular "blazer," his gray jockey cap, and the black coat which he seems to wear not because of its appropriateness to the rest of the costume but because he has it; shrewd, energetic, and like most nervous people, with a sharp, incisive voice. But the brook, bless you, doesn't mind that at all; it doesn't mind even the chattering red squirrels and the blue jays in the pines with voices as harsh as a rusty gate hinge. The brook keeps on blab, blab, blabbing to itself softly as a baby, not caring whether anyone listens to its sweet voice or not. The novelist would tell you that is what makes it so sweet to hear when anyone does stop to listen.

But the procession keeps marching along, big birds and little, all busy until the shadow of a hawk's wings frightens them into silence; gay orioles, testy as the Lords Baltimore whose livery they wear, sweeping past with a blaze of black and orange and the snap of wings; droll, big-headed fly-catchers that remind you of a boy you used to go to school with — the same boy whom you could beat seven times running at "four old cat,"[80] but who always outwitted you at "tag," the boy that is now a judge in the Supreme Court, while you are — no matter what; gay, little redstarts, so unlike in color that you never imagine they are mates; neat black and white creepers as trim as barbers' poles; grosbeaks with their breasts red as a pelican's in her piety. And how the trees have to be inspected by this keen-eyed crowd! Busy vireos travel along each limb, peering in every crack and warbling snatches from old songs; warblers of all kinds go round and round the branches, heartlessly tearing baby caterpillars out of their silken cradles; woodpeckers inspect the trunks by traveling upward, nuthatches repeat the operation in reverse order, so that, like Jack Spratt and his wife, [81] between them they leave nothing; and brown creepers search the ground over again, following a special direction round and round. What a company there is of them, each seeming to find plenty which the other has left behind, as if worms were a sort of heavenly manna to birds and increased by being fed on. But how do the poor worms manage to live? The professor, if you asked him, would talk to you for an hour about "the survival of the fittest" but you would best not mention the matter to him, for the birds

---

[80] Four Old Cat was a variation of round ball and Three Old Cat; games played in the 1800s. These ball games were the precursors to American baseball.
[81] Jack Sprat (or Spratt), a nursery rhyme from at least the seventeenth century. "Jack could eat no fat, His wife could eat no lean; But, together both, They licked the platter clean."

all believe in "natural selection," and they have an undoubted taste in worms.

There, now, across one of the shallows of the brooklet, walks a water wagtail,[82] walks, not hops, while a chewink[83] and a chipping sparrow sit on the fence to watch the feat and criticise his gait. A kingbird swings in the top of the apple tree; a catbird down in the alder bush is trying to make himself heard; and now, just as you are going off into a drowse and are ready to believe wonders, an animated windmill spins up to you, buzzing as if struck by a "norther." It is only a humming bird come to inspect. He frequents the place, for he knows a spot up the brook where the jewel weed hangs its golden horns among tender leaves, and he was on his way thither.

The windmill buzzes off again, but there is no more time to dream by the brooklet; for the world will no longer stay outside the happy valley, and the noon whistles, seconded by a ready response within, urge you to leave the brooklet. But it stays there still, and will be there long after you have ceased to visit it; and so long as it remains hard by the house where the poet lives, near to the novelist and not far from the professor (for it is so very small that it has now and then to remind itself of its own existence by these famous landmarks) — so long as it stays, the little birds will seek it early and it will be there, as now, a part of "Paradise" to all who know how to make the best of what this world gives.

— Fannie Pearson Hardy

---

[82] Wagtail birds received their name for their almost constant tail-feather wagging. They catch prey in shallow water.
[83] The chewink is a member of the finch family.

Illustrations by Walter Manly Hardy

XXII — Northern Maine

by
Anna Boynton Averill

My native wilds! for years untold,
The morning touched your hills with gold,
The north wind swept your fragrant glooms,
And bore the larch and pine perfumes
Across your lakes of lily blooms.

The fir, the hemlock and the pine
Sang on the heights; — and moss and vine
Made many a far, dim valley sweet
And shadowy for the shy fawn's feet.

In silvery solitudes the loon
Laughed with the echoes; and the moon
Made splendor on the mountains when
The Storm King slept, unseen of men.

O woods and lakes and wandering streams!
Ye have awakened from your dreams.
Your sweet breath blew abroad. Beware!
The gay world comes and finds you fair.

— Will all wild things take wing away?
I ween I would an' I were they.
Up these deep waterways I'd fare,
If I were wolf, or moose, or bear,
Or bird, or fawn, or fox, or hare!

O Northern wilds! you surely hold
In your great heart some refuge old,
Safe hid and far and deep and dumb,
Where the gay world can never come!

Cottontail Rabbit
(Editor's Collection)

XXIII — A Fire Of Poplar

Forest and Stream – February 6, 1890

A CHAQUE saint sa chandelle![84] Let every man worship at the shrine of his choosing! One believes in hickory, one in oak, and one in rock-maple, but whoever sung the praises of a poplar fire? If God made them to see the excellencies of these particular trees — for fire-building comes by instinct rather than by education, and no amount of science and rhetoric can induce a man to alter his preference or to change his style — if God made them thus, why may not some special power have been given me to see the virtues of the poplar?

It is true that there is little in its outward appearance to recommend this wood. Poplar, with its wide-angled, open boughs offer no concealment nor convenient crotches, and the birds will not nest in its branches; its sap has no sweetness; its wood has no beauty. There may be a prejudice against it too, because it is a cold tree and shivers even in the summer; but not many, certainly, would burn poplar from preference. There are those, not a few, who will tell you to take anything else sooner, even sheet iron and asbestos roofing; who will praise water-soaked ash and balm-of-gilead[85] and basswood in

---

[84] À chaque saint sa chandelle is a French phrase with a meaning such as, "Honor to whom honor is due."

[85] Balm of Gilead is a hybrid deciduous tree, also going by Balsam poplar. It was once used as a first aid salve.

comparison. And who will declare to you by the sacred relics of their own bitter experience, that one's cup of misery is not full until he has been forced to make camp in a rain storm and to build a poplar fire?

And a campfire it must be — if one is determined to disregard all good advice and to try the experiment — both from reasons of propinquity, because such poplar as is wanted does not effect the neighborhood of houses; and out of respect to the fire. That is, but half a fire which is not an object of solicitude and careful attention; whose wants are not noticed by watchful eyes and supplied by willing hands; whose pleasant warmth is received without gratitude, as "merely a mode of motion" with a mechanical equivalent in foot-pounds.

A fire should have an aesthetic as well as an economic value. "For the beauty of the honey and the good of the bees," said the wise old monk, who was also a successful apiarist, but no Benthamite,[86] and the man does not deserve a fire who will not consider its beauty as well as his own comfort. Strict utilitarianism is a poor inducement to lay golden eggs; as well be killed out of curiosity as forced to lay one's self to death out of cupidity, says the goose. And has no one ever noticed how the fire goes down when the kettle goes on? It is a lesson on the value of idealism — popular, not philosophic idealism, as opposed to materialism — which denies the unseen, and to utilitarianism (falsely so called) which sees not the thing, but the dollars in it.

---

[86] Benthamite, a person who supports the philosophical system of utilitarianism, the doctrine that an action is right if it promotes happiness, and that the greatest happiness of the greatest number should be the guiding principle of conduct.

The fire means thoughts and aspirations, the interchange of noble sentiments and the growth of nobler parts; wherefore, though all should end in smoke and ashes at last, let us treat the fire as something more than a convenience for cooking. Being of poplar, which most count worthless, there can be no gratification in its costliness or its rarity (which otherwise have reconciled many to discomfort and bitter food); and since it already bears an ill name, so that its faults are likely to outweigh its virtues — impressing us first — any pleasure which it affords should not be deemed subjective, but be attributed to an inherent worthiness in the wood, which by its own virtue renders us responsive.

And in the first place, green poplar will not burn; there your informant was right. It has its uses; it may be peeled and "driven" and converted into pulp at last, or it may be wrought into an ox yoke or a pitchfork handle or a canoe paddle, which, when seasoned, will compare with the birch, ash and rock maple articles in strength and elasticity; but if anyone wishes to see verdancy, viridity, greenness beyond compare, let him try to make a fire of the next greenest thing he can find, which will be the round limbs of a sapling poplar. Nor is the "down wood," as hunters call that which has fallen naturally, much better, being slimy beneath the rotting bark, heavy from moisture, and, as we say Down East,[87] "soggy."

---

[87] In Maine, the term "Down East," also as "Down East Maine" or "Downeast Maine," is the area of the state along the coast roughly between the Penobscot River and the border with Canada, including rural Hancock and Washington counties. A

As the camper out cannot wait for wood to season, he seems likely to forego the pleasure of a poplar fire unless there is some *via media* provided. It is an embarrassing question, but — do you know a poplar when you see it? Of course, not the gnarly, starveling pasture shrub which answers to that name, and the small-sized, jaundiced, angular sapling which spindles up among second-growth birches, but a first-class poplar in its prime, do you know *that*?

Poplar Tree – On a Maine Trail
(Editor's Collection)

It is rarely to be seen, if at all, outside the wilderness, and even there an apprentice at woodcraft would probably pass it by; for it grows large and tall, two feet, sometimes nearly three feet, in diameter, and so rough-barked that it might easily be mistaken for maple. Having reached a certain size it grows more slowly than pine, and the largest— among which may be

---

person from this area of Maine may be called a "down-easter." The word stems from nautical terminology referring to direction. It was also a type of clipper ship, which was the subject of the Billy Joel song, "The Downeaster Alexa."

counted some of the fine trees on the Passadumkeag — probably date back as far as the Mirimichi fire of 1825, which with the great Chase fire of the same year, swept across the State, planting birch and poplar where pine and hemlock had been.

A water-loving tree, it reaches its greatest perfection on the intervales by brook and riverside, either in clumps by itself or mingled with trees of almost every other kind. Having attained a good size and its maturity, it dies; and standing on year after year, growing drier and at the same time softer, it seasons itself and becomes the best campwood that the woods afford. To make a fire of poplar, use wood that has died on the stump.

The hunter or tourist who beaches his canoe near a grove of large poplars may say to himself that he has his firewood already cut, split and collected for him; for this task, which usually begins as soon as the tent has been raised and continues until the labor grows wearisome, or the night shades close about, is wonderfully lightened by the obliging poplar. He has only to pick out the dead trees or the tall stubs which remain standing, and if of small size and dry, he can push them from the stump with his hands; if larger and sound at the butt, there may be some hard chopping, for seasoned poplar is like horn;[88] but when the long trunk comes down with a mellow thrash — its own deadness muffling the echoes — and measures its length on solid earth at last, in most cases the shock proves too much for its decrepit age, and when it falls prostrate, there it lies broken into pieces convenient for camp use. Then what a

---

[88] The use of the word, *horn*, with wood represents hardness. *Hornbeam* wood is very hard, 'horn' meaning 'hard' and 'beam' being the name for a tree in old English.

sight is revealed! What a page in the history of once happy homes! Old nests come tumbling out of the chickadee vacant apartments, chip-dust sifts out of the woodpeckers' open doorways, and where the shattered trunk is cleft adown the center, all the arcana of their housekeeping stand revealed.

There are holes in all stages of construction — some unfinished, others wrought out to completion, with evident signs of occupancy, from which we can in fancy see the family of big-mouthed nestlings who grew up in dark and narrow quarters, but now are working in open air under the four winds. Some are small — the downy woodpecker's little domicile; and others, more capacious, belonged to the hairy; this great one which seems like a bird's boarding house, was the home of the golden-wing; and here on the outside the logcock has left his blaze.

Sometimes one finds in these dead trees the remains of a nest more interesting than any woodpecker's — that of the red bellied nuthatch, perhaps the most abundant of our woods' birds. The woods resound with their harsh, metallic, drawling tee eet, tee-eet, and they may be seen everywhere industriously running up and down the tree trunks, too busy to turn about, or else because nature shaped both ends alike, as indifferent to "end-for-ending" as a steam ferryboat. Their nest is a deep hole excavated by themselves, externally so much like a chickadee's or a downy woodpecker's that it might be passed unnoticed but for one peculiarity, the two nests which I have seen were both distinguishable and even noticeable on account of a considerable quantity of pitch which was smeared about the opening both above and below.[89] As one was in a white birch and the other in a poplar — trees which yield no gum nor resinous exudations — the busy little home makers must have made many a journey back and forth before they collected all the pitch which ornamented their lintel and doorposts, for it ran down like the ointment upon Aaron's beard.[90]

This dry poplar is a very light wood, lighter than dry cedar even, so that it is astonishing to see how large a piece a man can shoulder and carry into camp. Having arrived there, each must construct his fire after his own fancy; it is a craft in which no man ever learns anything or will consent to be taught of his neighbor. Ancient as the art is, going back to the shadowy, prehistoric ages when man was separated from the brutes and a brand given him as the sign of his superiority, it is as primitive as at first; a naked savage knows more about making a fire than the inhabitant of St. James', and the one who could not live on raw meat by a grim turn of fate is the one who would not know how to cook it. But everyone has his own

---

[89] One of these nests was empty, the other contained five eggs. They were described in *The Auk** at the time of their discovery, and are now in the collection of Mr. William Brewster, of Cambridge, Mass. The only other instance I have seen of a bird pitching its nest was a redstart, which built a wonderful little nest, but was too vain to hide it, so that the boys tore it down. But the note properly belongs to Miss Florence A. Merriam, and I believe, is mentioned in her delightful little volume, "Birds With an Opera Glass." (*The Auk was the scientific journal published by the American Ornithological Society. Now named, *Ornithology*. Eckstorm was a contributing writer.) (Ref. Original)

[90] From Psalm 133:2, "It is like the precious ointment upon the head, that ran down upon the beard, even Aaron's beard: that went down to the skirts of his garments." King James Bible.

theories of fire architecture; and you may name a man from the fire he builds, just as from the style of the nest you can determine the kind of bird that made it. One lays all his sticks across both andirons, and another will place a certain number with one end only resting on the dogs — each with convincing arguments in favor of the reasonableness of his own method; and I knew a man once, of kingly intellect, with a firm grasp on half the sciences and the power to make all the metals obey him, who to the day of his death placed his kindlings on the top of his pile in order to make the fire draw down.

Nevertheless, though the details differ, there are prevailing fashions in campfires. A woodsman of the old school stands agape, seeing for the first time one of the double fires which have become the mode of late. Intended to stand between two tents, pitched to face each other, these fires are long, narrow and made without back-logs. The hand-junks, which in the woods take the place of andirons, stand at a freezing distance apart, and wood of more than cord-wood length is piled upon them; two forked sticks, one at each end of the fire, support a long green pole, which takes the place of the old-fashioned crane and gives attachment to pot-hooks of various lengths and rude contrivance. These are generally made of a small green tree, cut below a fork and hung inverted over the fire, one prong being trimmed short, the other cut at a convenient length and furnished with a reverse hook for hanging the kettle, by driving in a nail near the end. For lack of a name they might be called *spunk-hungans*, after the now obsolete "lug-stick" or "spunk-hungans" of the lumbermen, which served the same purpose in the days when every camp was heated by an open fire.

Campfire Construction

In, *The Book of Camp-Lore and Woodcraft* (1920) Dan Beard (the founder of the first Boy Scouts Society) writes:

(The Camp-fire is) built with an eye to two purposes: one is to reflect heat into the open tent in front, and the other is to so construct it that it may last a long time. When one builds a camp-fire one wants to be able to roll up in one's blanket and sleep with the comforting conviction that the fire will last until morning.

The book includes the following images, which along with Eckstorm's description, will allow the reader to appreciate the endless combinations of *architecture* and the expounding statements from those who profess to prefer one setup versus another. In figure 97, the logs on the side are the hand-junks, or fire-dogs (in place of andirons) and in this setup, there are multiple backlogs.

Additional fire setups and hanging implements.

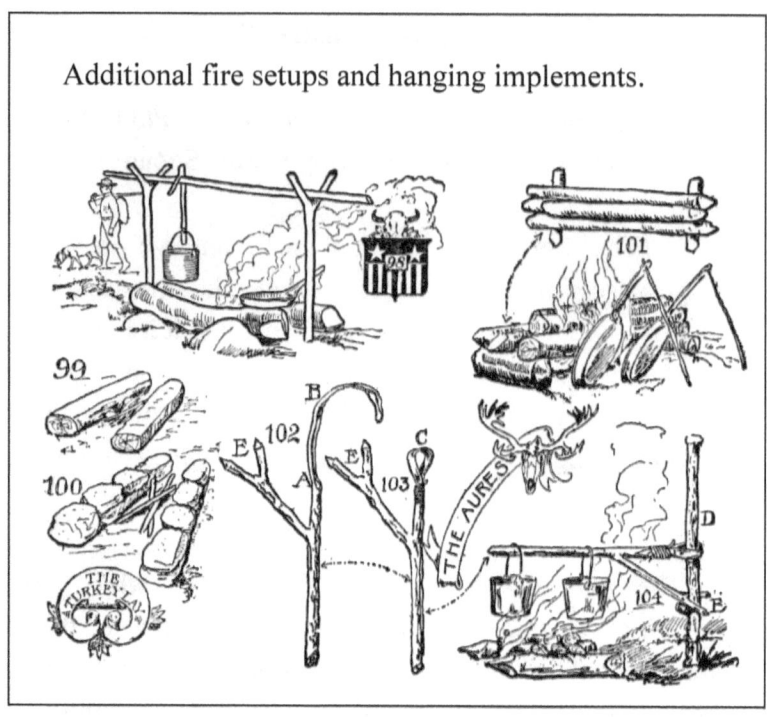

When deserted, campfires of this sort have a gallows-air which is not reassuring; and encountered on a carry with their blackened stakes and half-burned brands, they are hideously suggestive of Indian tortures and pictures of martyrdoms.

The regular hunter's fire is of quite another order. Its hand-junks approach each other socially, and a couple of back-logs of some wet or slow-wasting wood, staked up behind to reflect the heat, increase the air of coziness. The cooking arrangements which accompany are aboriginally simple. Of course, a "hook-stick" for lifting kettles on and off — which is only a miniature spunk-hungan without the nail — is always a necessity, but in addition, one or more straight green poles are all that is wanted. These, stuck into the ground or under a stone or tree root at such an angle as to bring the other end above the fire, support the kettle and may be adjusted at pleasure by placing a stone beneath the further end to raise, upon it to depress the pole.

It is the sign of a careful hunter always to remove his stew-pole from the fire when his cooking is finished. "Stew-pole" is the common name, but sometimes it is called a "spygelia"[91] — yet never that I knew by anyone who had not first heard the word on the Passadumkeag. How such terms arise and whither they vanish is a problem for the wise; but some are Indian, some few Scotch, some come from the Provinces, and some, with all the savor of their original saltness, are sea terms, completely naturalized in the forest. The woods have not so much an idiom as a vocabulary of their own, whose peculiarities are shibboleth to the ignorant, whether they talk or write. And yet for us who speak by nature of "drives," "jams," "peavies" and "wangans,"[92] because we know them by no other names and could not express the idea in other terms, there are not wanting those who accuse us of using too technical language.

This wood is the nonpareil for campfires. Although so light and so soft that it may be broken with fingers, it spends well and gives out a heat which makes it, for summer use at least, not inferior to maple. Its cracks and crevices expose a large surface to the fire, making the blaze strong and steady; and if

---

[91] In Dan Beard's book, noted earlier, this is spelled, speygelia-stick.

[92] Terms of the lumbermen and woodsmen. Log drives, log jams, peavey poles for grasping logs, and wangans (a number of uses in the lumberman's woods as company store, cache of equipment, or even a boat for lugging supplies).

a decorative style of fire-building is wished, the woodpeckers' holes can be used with effect.

For cooking, poplar has this advantage, that it can be broken into as small pieces as desired and fed to the fire slowly. And there is just at present a frizzling and a sizzling about the fire, which if not contradicting the assertion that it is not the whole duty of the fire to perform the cooking, demonstrates that this is its chief end. The coffee is boiling in its pail on one stew-pole and the potatoes on the other, while trout broiled and trout fried are making hot work for the cook.

We may call ourselves philosophers and affect to despise anything lower than mind, but it usually happens that when the call to supper comes the phenomenon of fried trout will outweigh all the noumena in existence; in other words, we ate, asking no metaphysical questions. It is not until we have eaten that we are really in condition to speculate on illimitable themes. The Omphalopsychites,[93] if they did not hit the truth they were after, may have travestied human nature more acutely than they knew, when they undertook to see God through the medium of their own stomachs; but this, at least, of the theory is true, that when the eyes are fixed, the mind is freest to swim in space.

The fire is always a worthy object for such contemplation: its unity in diversity, its constant change without transmutation hold the attention without distracting it. When supper is over and the camp work finished, one can lie back in perfect contentment, oblivious of the rest of creation. A bed of boughs

---

[93] Omphalopsychite, a name for the Hesychasts, the monks of the Middle Ages, from their habit of gazing upon the navel.

from which the strong heat draws the aroma of the fir, a headrest of interlocking hands or a blanket for a pillow, the tent above to keep off the dews and a fire in front, which for the night is the mathematical center of the universe — these are luxuries for which the soul may well be thankful.

The fire draws upward with a steady flame, brightening as the night grows darker and the stars come out one by one. It shines on the tree leaves overhead and moves them to a gentle fluttering by the current of hot air which it sends up; it lifts the shadows of the surrounding woods and sometimes lights the wings of a bat circling near. At times an Acadian owl may pass softly through the lighted space, or sit in the gloom just outside, making known its presence by one of its several noises. The best-known note is the saw-whetting, from which it gets its name of saw-whet owl; this closely resembles the sound of filing an "up-and-down" mill saw, set in a frame. It also makes a whining noise, and the soft conversational *co-co-co, co-co-co* already mentioned. Besides these, I am told of a note resembling the tinkling of small bells and of a harsh, nasal *ah-ah*. Indeed, I have myself heard at night in the woods a sharp, harsh noise — which I was told was made by the saw-whet — that resembled this as much as anything, but the heaviness of sleep interfered with scientific accuracy, and in my journal I find merely the comment: "Not knowing the other noises I did not remember this." This bird undoubtedly breeds in the woods north of Katahdin, but in the latitude of Bangor I have never seen one earlier than Oct. 19th nor later than March 21st. Between these dates they are not rare, being most frequently found in barns and outhouses, where they go for warmth and mice. What they eat when in the woods I do not know, never having seen one which did not appear half starved, nor having found the feathers of any small bird or any sign of their catching bird, mouse or shrew; but I have known four of them to be picked up dead, apparently from starvation.

The fire burns low. Pile on the wood and let us see it burn! 'Tis joy to watch such a fire. There is no uncertainty nor feeble flickering in its work, no bluster of roaring and lashing out of forked blue flames, which impart neither light nor heat. It rises clear, broad and yellow, steady as a candle and strong as if it fed on wax. This poplar gives itself without grudging — wood and fire are one — not as if it meant destruction to the wood, but a realization of good which otherwise would be truly lost. Is it better to rot or to burn? Oh, the calorie which lies locked up in wood and men, it might warm a world!

There is little smoke to this fire; that comes of half combustion — a wood which will not yield and a fire which is not strong enough to do its work. This is the true waste of a fire — not what is consumed, nor yet what remains, but what through inefficiency is lost. Smoke is discord, lack of adjustment; it is failure — to speak transcendentally. But the most plainly practical, to the millimeter-exact man whoever scoffed at esoteric meanings, would not deny that smoke can *produce* discord even in well-regulated families. It is not least among the merits of the poplar, then, that it does not smoke. Sparks and smoke are of one nature; but the first have an ardency which excuses the waste because it is the sign of strength; just as to the man of invention, driven by his yet untried ideas, to leave the piece of work on which he labors and begin another and another, the failure to finish the work in hand is forgiven because there is ability to accomplish greater.

Yet sparks are the airiest nothings, more unsubstantial than the smoke; restless and unsteady, they aspire only to die. It is their nature — as fixed as fate. The poet saw it long ago when he said that:

man was born unto trouble as the sparks fly upward —

or better in marginal reading,

"as the sons of the burning coal lift up to fly."
The sparks fly up, but the coals fall down.
"My words fly up," said the Danish King, "my thoughts remain below."

Why is it that words can be so divorced from what they represent? Why is it that the coals fall, but the sons of the burning coal rise up to fly? Are words, the children of thoughts, so light? And do thoughts gather ashes with age?
And why?

Pile on more wood!

These are but vain questions of the fire's breeding.

Pile on more wood!

If answers must be given,
let them come in sleep.
Draw in the tent,
spread down the blankets on the boughs,
and while the fire still glows outside,
lie down to sleep.

To sleep, perchance to dream.

— Fannie Pearson Hardy

The Dearest Bird

by
Anna Boynton Averill

This day of winter dark and drear,
The dearest bird of all the year
Comes freely to my window here
    With gleeful song that gladdens me.
Summer and winter, spring and fall,
I hear his cheery, merry call,
And O I love him best of all,
    My friendly little chickadee.

Alert and blithe, no cold benumbs
This dainty guest who daily comes
To dine upon his dole of crumbs
    And bring a world of joy to me;
Then gaily to the greenwood hies,
A speck of warmth in wintry skies,
A trusting heart in tiny guise,
    O, blessed little chickadee!

XXIV — Through The Heart Of Maine

by
Anna Boynton Averill

Down the dark gorge in rushing flight
  By frowning ridge and beetling scar,
We flash from darkness into light
  To break thy dream bright Onawa.

What wild and winged steed is this
  That through the rock's heart shrieking flies?
That leaps the tarn and deep abyss
  Below these blue October skies?

This path was torn by Titan might;
  The mountain rock was rent and flung
Down shuddering chasms left and right;
  From cliff to cliff these spans were hung,

And forests hurled apart to make
  A way for this swift steed to fly.
This blue bright morn his wings we take
  And wood and wave and peak go by.

His giant heart-beats thrill us through.
  — The poetry of motion this, —
Swift as the eagle skims the blue
  We pass the towering precipice

And thunder down the long defile.
  The bright woods flash away, and high
The purple mountains pile on pile
  Loom round us in the cloudless sky.

Stout heart, strong brain and steady hand
  Direct thy flight — we fear no ill.
Fly swifter yet, O, Giant grand!
  Thou canst not work thine utmost will!

To these thou bearest on thy wing
  This golden day hath no alloy.
The great woods shout, the caverns ring,
  Thine onward rush is rhythmic joy.

This poem is about the train that passes through Onawa, Maine. The towering precipice would be Borestone Mountain. In Averill's 1908 book, this photograph is included showing the mountain and the tracks.

XXV — Largely Personal – About Owls

Forest and Stream – January 23, 1890

IT IS night now, and in winter the night is for owls. In summer the small birds sometimes wake during the long hours; the chippy, as if roused from pleasant dreams, trills a little song before tucking her head under her wing; the vesper sparrow often sings a few clear notes; the whippoorwill chants in his vigils; and the loon, sailing on the moonlit lakes, lifts a long halloo, to which the hills respond. But when the winter's cold closes in at evening and the heavens stand dark blue and distant, and the stars blaze with a brilliancy unknown on warmer nights, what birds are there abroad but the owls?

Chickadees and nuthatches, grosbeaks and red-polls, long since made themselves comfortable on some sheltered limb, muffling their toes in their feathers; their enemies, the shrikes and hawks, did the same; the grouse, after his cold supper of poplar twigs, settled in the snow to wait for morning; but the owls are out all night. They whoop to each other; they break up rabbit parties and flying squirrel conventions; they scour the woods far and wide, bent on mischief, their coming first proclaimed by the silent blue shadow which glides before them. What mortal terror must chill the hare, frisking in the moonlight, as, affrighted at the shadow, he turns and sees those goggle-eyes glaring at him. The incident is so tragic, the moral so deep and universal, that it might be given a place in

Holbein's "Dance of Death,"[94] with the motto, "For man knoweth not his end."

Artists have never understood the nature of the horned owl or they would have appreciated his value as an emblem of evil — something a little better adapted to artistic representation than either Sin or the Devil, but containing the essence of both. The truth about him is best told as it was first told:

Time: thirty years ago.

Scene: two little girls playing school;

"Now, Alice, let's play definitions," says the elder to the younger.

Alice agrees.

"Now, Alice, I shall say 'What is an owl?' and you shall say, 'I don't know,' and I shall tell you."

After a moment for learning the lesson comes the question. "What is an owl?"

To which Alice responds with equal truth and ignorance:

"A owl is a beast."

A horned owl bears little resemblance to Minerva's bird[95] which was "accounted wise for saying nothing," nor to any of those other sad and gentle creatures which are represented as moping about church yards and complaining to the moon. He

---

[94] *The Dance of Death*, from the German artist Hans Holbein (c. 1497 – 1543), is given in a series of detail scenes done in woodcuts where *death* visits unsuspecting people from various levels of society.

[95] Minerva, is the Roman association to Athena, the virgin goddess of wisdom, who was often accompanied by a small owl, a symbol that has been depicted in the Western world as representing knowledge and wisdom.

is a fiend incarnate. He harries all the smaller animals with relentless cruelty, and all night long he howls and hoots in the swamps, making horrid noises in great variety.

"I was not born in the woods to be scared by an owl," says the proverb, but the best hunter alive will probably remember at least one time in his life when he has wished himself somewhere else, all on account of an owl.

These creatures seem to me uncanny: a monkey, because with all his man-likeness he falls so far short of humanity; a parrot, because with a thimbleful of brains its wit puts man's in dis-esteem; and the horned owl, because without a drop of the milk of human kindness, he seems to read men's thoughts and to impute base motives.

And yet I once loved a horned owl. A farmer brought him to the door and I purchased the bird for a private investment. Indeed, from the moment I first saw him, he was mine; there was something fine and commanding about the creature which won my admiration. 1 always spoke of the bird as "him" out of deference to its spirit — braver bird there never was — although its great size and the pure white collar about the neck showed that it was a female.

He had been trapped and was hurt; he had been caged and was offended; he was wild from the woods and wholly unused to civilization, but when I lifted him from his box and placed him on the floor, wholly unconfined, he made no attempt to escape, and showed neither fear nor resentment. His great eyes scanned each one of us narrowly, but he stood as unmoved as a captive Indian. From the very first he manifested a preference for me, and before night he learned to distinguish my step from all others. When anyone else came near his box he would snap his bill loudly, but at my approach he was always silent. He seemed to enjoy having me handle him; would let me take all sorts of liberties with his feathers, even to examining his ears. He would lie quietly upon his back and let me carry him about on my arm; and he especially enjoyed having his head scratched. When I rubbed it gently with my finger, working the feathers back and forth, he would sit with half-closed eyes showing his pleasure by the relaxation of his muscles and the slow movements of his inner eyelids. He never made an attempt to escape or to bite.

Whether he would have used his claws can only be conjectured, for I always held both feet when I handled him for fear he might forget his manners; but as I once went into a dark room whither he had escaped from his box, and recaptured him without receiving a scratch, it seems probable that his intentions were good. If the best of its kind is the fittest to survive, that owl should be alive today. How his demise came about need not be related, and which cried the more over it, the owl or myself, the owl will not now tell.

The next which came was also a horned owl, a little black fellow, as ugly as wickedness. A missionary preparing for work among the Cannibal Islanders might have learned the ways of heathendom from the little brute. To be sure he had his griefs; his wings had been clipped and his nails cut; his leg was sore from the trap, and his temper completely ruined by weeks of captivity, but so much diabolism could never have been wholly acquired since the date of his misfortunes. I handled him as I pleased, but it was through no good will of his; indeed, he seemed greatly provoked whenever I tucked him under my arm and carried him about. It was funny to see him try to get away when put down, flapping with his wings and hobbling on his knuckle joints, with his toes turned under like a Chinese woman's[96] and his head facing squarely between his shoulders. It is funny also to remember how I went to visit him in the morning and found only an empty box, while from the top of a very high wood pile he looked down on me, grotesquely like some of Cimabue's angels.[97] But this escape and the mischief which he did during that night of liberty so filled the measure of his crimes that he never saw another morning.[98]

The great popular superstition regarding owls seems to be that of their inability to see in the daytime. It is probable that the desire to account for the mysterious nictitating lid has been strong enough to outweigh all other evidence against this theory. What the use of this membrane is I cannot say, but that it is intended to shield the eyes from too strong light seems very doubtful; for, however bright the light, when intent on watching anything, the lid is withdrawn. One has but to notice the great contractility of the owl's iris and the peculiar shape of the eyeball, which makes it an optical instrument with remarkable power of adjustment to a focus, to believe that it is an eye especially formed for keen seeing in light as well as in darkness. And the facts bear out the belief. Even the barred owl can see well in the daytime, and a close observer tells me

---

[96] This is in reference to foot binding, a practice that only ended in the early 20th century.

[97] Cimabue c. 1240 – 1302 was an Italian painter. Depending on your view of his art, and whether appreciating his *Maestà* or *Santa Trinita Maestà*, you may agree with Eckstorm's classification as, "grotesquely *like some*."

[98] At the end of this chapter there is a letter from Manly Hardy on the "size and power of owls," in which he mentions one that killed a goose. It could be, *this* was that owl.

that he never saw a horned owl which had not first seen him. He states also that they can distinguish the motion of raising a rifle as far off as he cares to shoot at them, which would seem to indicate that their eyesight, if defective — as most of the books believe — is so for astronomical distances only.

The only one of our Northern owls which seems shortsighted is the little Acadian owl. It is more exclusively nocturnal than any other that we have here, seldom, if ever, moving in the daytime unless disturbed. When found it can often be taken alive without difficulty. But whether this unwariness is due to defective sight remains to be proved, for those which we have had as pets seemed to see perfectly in the daytime, although they did not become lively until night.

In all we have had three Acadian owls. One refused all food and was liberated after a few days; the second ate only too willingly and died from devouring a scrap of salted meat; the other was for a long time a most interesting pet, although this was before my remembrance. Father tells me, he was given the range of the house, and soon became very tame, on good terms with the whole family except the cat. He was a gentle little creature, quiet in the daytime, but lively at night, when he would sometimes be heard talking to himself — the only vocal noise that he made — a soft co-co-co, co-co-co several times repeated. He seemed to notice vertical movements more than horizontal ones, perhaps because he saw the shadow quicker, perhaps on account of the arrangement and structure of his eyes, which are almost immovable and have a vertical contracting pupil, like a cat's. He never was contented to sit on any perch which would cause one foot to be below the other, and whenever he alighted on such a place (as the top of a clock or a chair back) he immediately walked sidewise up the incline until he stood at the highest point, where his feet could be on a level.

He was an acrobat in a small way, for when a small stick was put between his jaws and he lifted by it, he would swing back and forth in wider and wider arcs until on some backward swing longer than the others, he could throw up his feet and grasp the stick, when he would raise himself into an upright position and look as sedate as any owl. His great delight was to torment the cat. He hectored the poor beast until an undisturbed nap was something only to be dreamed of, flying down from some high perch with a speed and silence which enabled him to scratch his victim's nose or ears and escape in good season. So sudden were the attacks that the cat got no opportunity of revenge until after the owl died and was mounted, when one day he tore off the owl's head. Whether he was satisfied that the bird was killed or was disgusted to find him only tow[99] and feathers can never be known; but after that he looked at the owl and the owl looked at him without enmity.

These notes are personal to an unusual degree, and perhaps should be called gossip rather than science. As the subjects are all dead, they cannot object to anything which has been said of them, and I am willing to vouch for its truth; but if anyone were to ask what the story teaches, a wiser man must tell him or else he must go directly to the owls.

— Fannie Pearson Hardy

---

[99] Tow – taxidermist stuffing; made from hemp, flax, cotton batting, etc.

The following letter to the editor appeared in the May 20, 1905 issue of *Forest and Stream*. A reader, Forked Deer (*letters to Forest and Stream were often signed with imaginative names*) from Oakland, California posed the following questions about the size of owls. The editors responded in that issue, and Manly Hardy offered his expertise as well.

The reader "Forked Deer," offers his thank you to the contributors on the subject with high praise for the father and daughter by the name of Hardy. He also makes mention of the editorial controversy on 'steel-shod poles,' that Mr. Hardy weighed in on two years prior. A summary of that historical information is included in this book, for which the reader will encounter shortly.

Size and Power of Owls

OAKLAND, Cal., April 18 — Editor *Forest and Stream*:

I have on several occasions seen in articles in the *Forest and Stream* mention made of an owl found in certain sections, notably that formerly known as the southwest, that from the description seemed to be larger than the great horned owl, which was formerly found over nearly the whole of our country and which I had always supposed was the largest North American species. One writer speaks of it as the eagle owl. Is the eagle owl found anywhere in the United States? Another writer from the cypress swamps of the South tells of one with a wing spread of six feet that easily picked up a full-grown mallard drake out of the water and flew away with it. Now, I am fairly familiar with the great horned owl, but I never saw one that measured even five feet across the wings, or that could possibly fly away with a full-grown mallard. While it is possible that the great northern snowy owl might be able to do this, that bird, I believe, never gets as far south as the section referred to, and it is quite certain, for other reasons, that it is not the bird referred to.

Can the *Forest and Stream* throw any light upon the subject?

— Forked Deer.

The Editor of *Forest and Stream* replied:

We fancy that the size and strength of the bird referred to as having a spread of six feet and being able to fly off with a full-grown duck, were overestimated. The eagle owl is a bird of Europe, not found in North America. The three greatest of our owls are the great horned, great gray and white or snowy. These are all about the same size, the last averaging the largest. None of them much, if at all, exceed five feet in their extent. At the same time, they are powerful birds. The great horned owl has been known to kill skunks and cats, and the other large owls are said to kill grouse, while the eagle owl of Europe is reported to attack fawns. Of course, a much larger bird or animal might be killed than could be raised from the ground and flown away with.

Manly Hardy replies:

Size and Power of Owls — May 27, 1905

Editor Forest and Stream:

Referring to an article on this subject in *Forest and Stream* of May 20, I would say that we have no eagle owls in North America, our largest being the great horned and the snowy. I have measured a good many of the great horned, and the largest spread four feet nine inches — four and one-half feet is the usual spread of a full-grown great horned owl. I have shot one having a full-grown rabbit in his claws — not the little cotton-tail, but one of our large northern hares.

I have known of several cases where they have carried off house cats. In one instance it was a very large cat. As a large cat will weigh near ten pounds, I should think it a very easy matter for one to carry off a mallard duck. I know that they can and do carry off our dusky ducks — which are about as heavy. I have seen the barred owl, which is much smaller and weaker, fly with a full-grown ruffed grouse with apparently very little exertion.

I once had a great horned owl mounted which had just killed a full-grown goose, and it is a very common thing for them to kill skunks. While their size is often greatly overstated, I can testify that they have considerable lifting power, as I once had one jerk my head up suddenly as I lay rolled up in a blanket. My hat had fallen off and he probably seized me by mistake thinking my head was a rabbit.

— Manly Hardy

The writer of the original letter, Forked Deer, wrote again to thank those who replied to his question.

He wrote, in part:

> OAKLAND, CAL., June 19 — I know of no source of information more satisfactory than the *Forest and Stream* in its own particular field. In the multitude of its readers are to be found manly sportsmen of the highest class, whose knowledge is for the most part derived from their own experience. It is true that even the experts differ sometimes on quite important matters. See the clink of steel-shod poles.
>
> Therefore. when I wrote the owl letter of inquiry I felt fairly sure it would elicit a satisfactory solution to the whole matter, and I was not disappointed — the editorial furnished the general details required; Mr. Hardy, who with his amiable and gifted daughter, I rank with the most reliable of your contributors, gave his personal experience.

It is with a letter such as this that illustrates the impact and impressions the father–daughter team of Manly Hardy and Fannie Hardy Eckstorm had on sportsmen across the country.

In his thank you letter Forked Deer also made reference to a series of letters that appeared in the magazine two years prior, dealing with in part, steel shod canoe poles, and other ways of the Maine woods. The controversy started from a Rudyard Kipling poem and once again, Manly Hardy offered his woods expertise. This topic is covered in the next chapter.

On the Hardy Bird Collection

Over 2,000 of Manly Hardy's 3,300 mounted specimens were purchased in 1913 for the City of Providence's (Rhode Island) museum by the Audubon Society for the sum of $5,000.

Before the shipment of the bird collection, the Hardy family held an open house for the local residents. The arrival to the museum, was frontpage news in the Providence Journal.

The journal *Science* reported, "The city will erect an addition to the museum almost as large as the present structure, equipped to exhibit the collections." The article continued, "The Manly Hardy collection of North American birds, ..., is one of the most valuable private collections in existence and represents thirty-three consecutive years of work on the part of Mr. Hardy and his daughter, Mrs. Fannie Hardy Eckstorm."

In 2013, Marilyn Massaro, Curator of Collections for the Museum wrote about the Hardy collection:

"From diminutive hummingbirds to regal raptors and California condors, the Manly Hardy Bird collection spans the full systematic range of North American species. It also includes a wide array of birds of paradise species, a favorite of Hardy's. Due to its antiquarian vintage, the collection also includes many extinct and endangered birds, including Carolina parakeets, ivory-billed woodpeckers, California condors, and a heath hen from Martha's Vineyard. This assemblage of so many species quickly became the core of the Museum's bird collection, as it remains to this day. Hardy built his collection primarily by purchase and exchange, though the birds from Brewer he collected and mounted himself."

The collection is available for researchers at the Museum of Natural History and Planetarium Roger Williams Park, Providence, Rhode Island. In addition, specimens from Hardy's collection are available in ongoing public exhibits, including his *Birds of Paradise* and *Wandering Albatross* in the Museum's Circle of the Sea (Oceania) gallery

Information for this note was sourced from the following:

1. "Hardy's Bird Collection, 100 Years in Providence," by Marilyn Massaro, Curator of Collections Museum of Natural History and Planetarium Roger Williams Park, Providence, Rhode Island. (Posted on February 11, 2013 https://rinhs.org/animals/manlyhardy100/)

2. Science, "Scientific Notes and News." New Series, Vol. 37, No. 946 (Feb. 14, 1913), pp. 249-252.

Juvenile Broad-Winged Hawk
(Editor's Collection)

XXVI — Owl And Chickadee

by

Anna Boynton Averill

A Fable for Reformers

The drowsy owl in the shadow sits
   Somber and silent, all day long,
Deep in the wood where the chickadee flits,
   Caroling gaily her gleeful song.

"Why do you bustle and chatter all day,
   Flying about with the sun in your eyes?"
Says the owl to the chickadee. "Try my way,
   And change your habits as I advise.

Adopt a diet of mouse and wren,
   Try to be sober and seem more wise,
Retire by day from the haunts of men
   And cultivate silence, and rest your eyes.

Forage in darkness with muffled flight,
   Then if you'll practice my loud 'Tu whoo,'
You can curdle men's blood in the dead of night
   And pass for a bear as I often do.

Follow these rules and be grumpy and sleep
   Summer and winter, and you will be
Esteemed for wisdom, accounted 'deep'!
   Why, I am an emblem! Look at me!"

But he hears, as he stares through the shadows gray,
   To see how impressed his hearer must be,
Out in the sunshine far away,
   Only a jubilant "chickadee dee!"

Black-capped Chickadee
(Editor's Collection)

XXVII — Red Gods

‡‡

In 1903 Forest and Stream published an editorial type essay from Mr. L. F. Brown, of Sand Lake, Michigan, who offered a critique of Rudyard Kipling's 1897 poem, "The Feet of the Young Men." This certainly is not one of Kipling's most widely known works, but was a tribute to the sportsmen and nature the world over. In the verse, Kipling, covers a great many scenes of the rituals of hunting. Letters to the editor were published for a year in response to Mr. Brown's perspective. At one point, the editors called a truce, to put the issue to bed, but they could not; letters continued to appear on the pages. The controversy is too long and involved to cover in this book. Mr. Brown's critique is required reading prior to the response from Manly Hardy, who gives his Maine woods expertise and his wider range view of the meaning of the poem for the benefit of the *Forest and Stream* readers.

‡‡

Forest and Stream - September 09, 1903
Some Musings at Sand Lake, Mich.

Spurious Writings About Angling and Nature.

It is astounding that so much counterfeit writing about sport and nature passes for super-excellent work. Some writers actually boast of their blindness to nature's beauty and grace, and secure admiration as "realists." Worse, other writers rhapsodize about that beauty in the language of the blind, while their own writing convicts them of not having visited the scenes they misdescribe.

For example, here is an extract from a much-exploited poem by Kipling:[100]

"Do you know the blackened timber? Do you know that racing stream,

With the raw, right-angled log-jam at the end,

And the bar of sun-warmed shingle, where a man may bask and dream

To the click of shod canoe poles round the bend?

It is there that we are going with our rods and reels and traces,

To a silent, smoky Indian that we know;

To a couch of new-pulled hemlock, with the starlight on our faces,

For the Red Gods call us out, and we must go."

The real log-jam consists of the mistruth and inexactness in this double quatrain. Stripped of its rhythm-tinsel, that "poetry" is to true nature-love and insight, what a daubed chromo-picture is to a painting by Turner. By what poetic license can readers be

---

[100] L. F. Brown does not give the name of the Kipling poem in his letter. It is "The Feet of the Young Men," first published in 1897. The full poem is included at the end of the chapter.

supposed to "know" some unlocated "blackened timber,"[101] and "that racing stream?"

No actual log-jam is "raw," right-angled," or "at the end" of such a stream. It is a wonderful study of hues — browns, umbers, faint pinks and purples, and dull reds and yellows, silver of lichens and green and crimson of mosses. Not one canoe-pole in a thousand in either the United States, India (outside of army equipment), Norway, British Columbia, or any of the Maritime Provinces of Canada, is "shod;" and when it is, it does not "click;" and if it did, even its impact on rocks "round the bend" would not be heard along quiet water, much less in the tumult and uproar of "that racing stream." Thus the falsehood makes the whole word-picture an affront to correct taste. Any megaphone "word-artist" can fling a potful of language-paint at a canvas; but it is reserved for some Quack of Error to demand that the resulting rent and hole in the canvas, and the "splotteration" that surrounds and befouls it, shall pass current for a magnificent picture, "tender, grand, and true!"

It would be difficult to place more false description in a like number of words than that contained in those eight lines of "poetry."

---

[101] In, *Exploring the Maine Woods – The Hardy Family Expedition to the Machias Lakes*, Fannie Hardy describes a pile of wood her father had left from a prior trip that had blackened and moldered. Likewise, many woodsmen will know of areas ravaged by fire, the black timber standing guard over the new growth.

Brown goes on:

Finally, note the rough, bungling words, "It is there that we are going," in the above citation from Kipling, and the pompous conceit of the words, "Red Gods!" What a credit and honor he deems it that he is possessed of those crimson deities! What a triumph of absurdity to give such a name to the heart-longing, so natural, simple and beneficent, to be right with Nature.

The word "traces" is meaningless — an Anglicism that refers to a section of spinning tackle that is never used on "racing streams;" so "traces" is misused as a rhyme for "faces." An Indian is not "smoky," but dark-skinned. Real canoeists and anglers who are sportsmen would not "go" to the Indian, but to the stream.

A "bar" is always a deposit of alluvium earth-sediment which has gathered and formed a mud bank or island. There never was a "bar" of "shingle," for that is very coarse gravel or small, water-worn stones to which the word "bar" cannot be correctly applied. (See Standard Dictionary for definitions of these words.) No sportsman would dream of sitting or reclining on such a hard, hot, uncomfortable seat as "sun-warmed shingle." "Bask and dream!" The real words should have been "bake and steam." Neither do campers sleep on a "couch" (bed) of hemlock twigs if they can get spruce boughs; and when they do, there is no "starlight on their faces." They "bask" in that as they smoke on some moss-covered log beside lake or stream.

In short, that rhyming is mere fakir vociferation, squawking of a brood-goose on addled eggs, self-conscious, mountebank strut and posing, brazen assumption by ignorance of real truth, insight, and knowledge, bawling claim to Nature-photography, vivid, "picturesque" word-painting and virile rhyme-gospel by a wonderful, "versatile" seer.

— L. F. Brown.

Manly Hardy Responds

There were many responses to Brown's letter over the following months published in *Forest and Stream*. It seems to have been an amusing topic for the editors of that magazine. Manly Hardy was one of the first to provide his thoughts. As far as can be determined, one letter rebuffed Hardy's response in support of Brown, while a dozen or so responded with their views in support of and aligned to Hardy's.

The controversy itself is not important. The purpose of including the above letter, and the response from Hardy, is for illustration of the woodlore history that is contained in Kipling's poem in relation to Hardy's lifelong Maine woods experiences.

Forest and Stream - October 10, 1903 (Vol. 61 Iss. 15)

Another View of Kipling's Poetry.

Editor Forest and Stream:

In your issue of September 26, Mr. L. F. Brown criticizes Kipling's verses:

> *"Do you know the blackened timber? Do you know that racing stream?*
> *With the raw, right-angled log-jam at the end,*
> *And the bar of sun-warmed shingle, where a man may bask and dream,*
> *To the click of shod canoe poles round the bend?"*

For sixty years I have been familiar with the scenes Mr. Kipling is describing, and I thought when I first read it, and still think the same, that there is no description in the English language which so vividly, briefly and truthfully tells the story of logs and water. It is true in every detail to what may be seen in Maine any year. How many places of "blackened timber" I remember, and "racing streams" is the exact term for many streams in Maine and New Brunswick.

Mr. Brown says that "no actual log-jam is 'raw,' 'right-angled,' of 'at the end' of such a stream." Anyone who has ever seen drives of logs has seen many places where they jam below a short bend and give the appearance of cutting off the stream completely. The two photographs which I enclose, though not typical of such jams, show the tendency of the logs to rear up at right angles. The word "raw" is just the word to use for such a scene, using it, after Webster, as "not altered from the natural state." The color which one sees in any scene depends so much upon the sensitiveness of the individual that no one could object if a man made out all the colors of the rainbow; but as to the "silver of lichens and green and crimson of mosses" they simply do not exist on a log-jam. The logs are driven the first year they are cut, and they grow no moss on their way down our rivers. If by chance a jam has to be left over one season it must be cleared away the next to let the next cut of logs through, and in case of even the most stubborn obstruction, the bark simply peels off, leaving a smooth, shining surface, which, washed by rain and seared by the suns of summer, offers no encouragement to "green and crimson mosses."

Mr. Brown objects to the "click of shod canoe-poles round the bend," asserting that, "not one canoe-pole in a thousand in either the United States, India (outside of army equipment), Norway, British Columbia, or any of the maritime provinces of Canada, is 'shod'; and when it is, it does not 'click'; and if it did, even its impact on rocks 'round the bend' would not be heard along quiet water, much less in the tumult and uproar of that 'racing stream.'"

The odd circumstance here is that Mr. Kipling is right and Mr. Brown is wrong on every point. I have seen hundreds of setting-poles in Maine, and I have yet to see the first one which was not shod, except in cases where a shod pole had been broken and a makeshift was used till a better could be procured. In the Provinces I have seen poles both "shod" and "barefoot," but the latter were used only because their owners were too poor to buy irons. Then the "click" of a pole telegraphs like the rattle of railroad iron. It can usually be heard from fifty to a hundred yards at the least, unless there is a strong wind blowing, or it is very rough water. I have hundreds of times heard the click of the poles long before the canoe came in sight round the bend. It can often be heard above the roar of the water nearly as far as one's voice could be heard. To anyone who has been in a canoe in quick water the "click" of a shod pole is as familiar as the sound of an oar in a rowlock is to a boatman.

Mr. Brown objects to the Indian being called "smoky"; it is the precise word. In my early childhood we used to have from ten to twenty Indian visitors in a day. Living in smoky camps as they did, their clothes were saturated with the smoke, and, with one's eyes shut, one could have told when there was an Indian in the room. In another way, too, they were "smoky." The smoke darkened their skins. I have often seen white men who, from living in smoky camps, had grown much darker from the smoke-tan.[102]

(Brown writes,) "Real canoeists and anglers who are sportsmen would not "go" to the Indian, but to the stream." But if the Indian was needed to handle the canoe they would probably have to go to the Indian. My experience with Indians has been like Brigham Young's when he sent for Ben Simonds to come and see him, and got for an answer: "When Indian want Brigham, Indian go Brigham. When Brigham want

---

[102] In her book, *Mothers of Maine*, Helen Coffin Beedy speaks of "dusky mothers," referring to the Indian mothers with their darker skin. Whether the color observed was from pigments or smoke dusk, the poem is a poem and open to the readers interpretation and thoughts.

Indian, Brigham come Indian."[103] If one wants an Indian, he goes to the Indian.

As for the statements that, "a bar is always a deposit of alluvium earth-sediment which has gathered and formed a mud bank or island," and, "there never was a "bar" of "shingle," for that is very coarse gravel or small, water-worn stones to which the word "bar" cannot be correctly applied," I must sorrowfully assert from much experience in running upon them, that we have the thing even if we do not know the name of it. But as for that matter, the Century Dictionary, if it may be fairly pitted against the Standard—which seems to be Mr. Brown's authority — not only covers this ground definition (2) of "bar," as "anything which obstructs"; but under [definition] 4(a) it expressly states that a bar is "a bank of sand, gravel or earth forming a shoal in any body of water." In our swift streams and rivers a bar of mud or fine sand cannot form in most places; only the heavy pebbles can withstand the current. The idea of basking and dreaming "on the bar of sun-warmed shingle" which Mr. Brown ridicules brings up very pleasant recollections to woodsmen. It is a very common thing when tired of poling upstream to haul the canoe out on a gravel bar and lie and bask in the warm sun. (Brown continues,) "Neither do campers sleep on a couch (bed) of hemlock twigs if they can get spruce boughs; and when they do there is no 'starlight on their faces.'"

Now, no man but a greenhorn ever uses spruce boughs to bough down with if he can get anything better; and every other

---

[103] Unverified quote. Simonds was known as Ben, Benj, or James Simonds. He was a trader with Brigham Young.

evergreen is better.[104] Fir is most generally used because it is commonly the easiest to get; but hemlock is fully as good. Fir, hemlock, cedar and even pine are preferred to the stiff boughs and prickly needles of the spruce. And as to the "starlight on one's face," one has missed something out of life who does not know what it is to lie out without cover. I can recall many nights, when I had no tent above me but the stars.

I would not wish to make any animadversions upon Mr. Brown's criticisms of woods life if I understood that he was confining himself to the region he knows; but I thought it was a general criticism of Mr. Kipling's poem, and I have yet to hear that Mr. Kipling was writing about Sand Lake, Michigan.

If Mr. Kipling had been foresighted enough to label it "Maine" or "Canada," there is no question he might have been passed *summa cum laude* on every point.

— Manly Hardy
Brewer, Maine

---

[104] In his entry of August 1, in *The Maine Woods*, Thoreau wrote, "We camped about two miles below Nickatow, on the south side of the West Branch, covering with fresh twigs the whithered bed of a former traveler. We could not get fir twigs for our bed here, and the spruce was harsh in comparison, having more twig in proportion to its leaf, but we improvised it somewhat with hemlock."

XXVIII — The Feet of the Young Men

Rudyard Kipling
1897

Now the Four-way Lodge is opened, now the Hunting Winds
are loose —
Now the Smokes of Spring go up to clear the brain;
Now the Young Men's hearts are troubled for the whisper of the
Trues,
Now the Red Gods make their medicine again!
Who hath seen the beaver busied? Who hath watched the black-
tail mating?
Who hath lain alone to hear the wild-goose cry'
Who hath worked the chosen water where the ouananiche is
waiting,
Or the sea-trout's jumping-crazy for the fly?

He must go — go — go away from here!
On the other side the world he's overdue.
'Send your road is clear before you where the old Spring-fret
comes o'er you,
And the Red Gods call for you!

So for one the wet sail arching through the rainbow-round the
bow,
And for one the creak of snow-shoes on the crust;
And for one the lakeside lilies where the bull-moose waits the
cow,
And for one the mule-train coughing in the dust.
Who hath smelt smelt-smoke at twilight? Who hath heard the
birch-log burning?
Who is quick to read the noises of the night?
Let him follow with the others for the Young Men's feet are
turning
Too the camps of proved desire and known delight!

Let him go — go — go away from here!
On the other side the world he's overdue.
'Send your road is clear before you where the old Spring-fret
comes o'er you,
And the Red Gods call for you!

I

Do you know the blackened timber — do you know that racing
stream
With the raw, right-angled log-jam at the end;
And the bar of sun-warmed shingle where a man may bask and
dream
To the click of shod canoe-poles round the bend'
It is there that we are going with our rods and reels and traces,
To a silent, smoky Indian that we know —
To a couch of new-pulled hemlock, with the starlight on our
faces,
For the Red Gods call us out and we must go!

They must go — go — go away from here!
On the other side the world he's overdue.
'Send your road is clear before you where the old Spring-fret
comes o'er you,
And the Red Gods call for you!

II

Do you know the shallow Baltic where the seas are steep and
short,
Where the bluff, lee-boarded fishing-luggers ride?
Do you know the joy of threshing leagues to leeward of your
port
On a coast you've lost the chart of overside?

It is there that I am going, with an extra hand to bale her —
Just one able 'long-shore loafer that I know.
He can take his chance of drowning, while I sail and sail and
sail her,
For the Red Gods call me out and I must go!

He must go — go — go away from here!
On the other side the world he's overdue.
'Send your road is clear before you where the old Spring-fret
comes o'er you,
And the Red Gods call for you!

III

Do you know the pile-built village where the sago-dealers trade
—
Do you know the reek of fish and wet bamboo?
Do you know the steaming stillness of the orchid-scented glade
When the blazoned, bird-winged butterflies flap through?
It is there that I am going with my camphor, net, and boxes,
To a gentle, yellow pirate that I know —
To my little wailing lemurs, to my palms and flying-foxes,
For the Red Gods call me out and I must go!

He must go — go — go away from here!
On the other side the world he's overdue.
'Send your road is clear before you where the old Spring-fret
comes o'er you,
And the Red Gods call for you!

IV

Do you know the world's white roof-tree — do you know that
windy rift
Where the baffling mountain-eddies chop and change?
Do you know the long day's patience, belly-down on frozen
drift,
While the head of heads is feeding out of range?
It is there that I am going, where the boulders and the snow lie,
With a trusty, nimble tracker that I know.
I have sworn an oath, to keep it on the Horns of Ovis Poli,
And the Red Gods call me out and I must go!

He must go — go — go away from here!
On the other side the world he's overdue.
'Send your road is clear before you where the old Spring-fret
comes o'er you,
And the Red Gods call for you!

How the Four-way Lodge is opened — now the Smokes of
Council rise —
Pleasant smokes, ere yet 'twixt trail and trail they choose —
Now the girths and ropes are tested: now they pack their last
supplies:
Now our Young Men go to dance before the Trues!
Who shall meet them at those altars — who shall light them to
that shrine?
Velvet-footed, who shall guide them to their goal?
Unto each the voice and vision: unto each his spoor and sign —
Lonely mountain in the Northland, misty sweat-bath 'neath the
Line —
And to each a man that knows his naked soul!

White or yellow, black or copper, he is waiting, as a lover,
Smoke of funnel, dust of hooves, or beat of train —
Where the high grass hides the horseman or the glaring flats
discover —
Where the steamer hails the landing, or the surf-boat brings the
rover —
Where the rails run out in sand-rift . . . Quick! ah, heave the
camp-kit over,
For the Red Gods make their medicine again!

And we go — go — go away from here!
On the other side the world we're overdue!
'Send the road is clear before you when the old Spring-fret
comes o'er you,
And the Red Gods call for you!

Notes:

— Four-way Lodge is the connection of east with fire, west
with water, south with air, and north with earth.

— The Red Gods are the spirits of the hunting grounds
waking man up in the spring.

— Ouananiche are landlocked salmon.

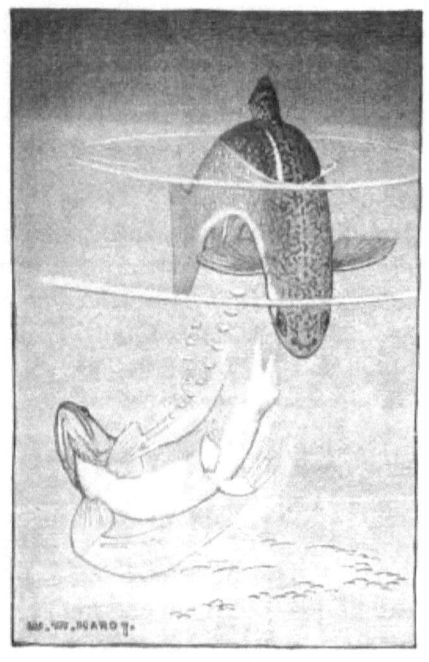

Illustration by Walter Manly Hardy

XXIX — On Not Getting Lost in the Woods

Forest and Stream – November 18, 1905

WE often see articles in the sporting papers giving people who are lost in the woods instruction as to how to find their way. It is very doubtful whether any of those who are so ready to tell others what to do, ever traveled much in the woods, and it is certain that, if lost there, they could never find their way by any of the so-called helps they offer to others. I have never known of anyone writing an article showing insane people how to become sane; but it is just as reasonable as telling those who are lost in the woods how to find their way out, for when a man is really lost he is practically insane and incapable of reasoning as he would be at other times, and even when he gets to well-known roads and clearings he does not recognize them. Men will often turn nearly, or quite, squarely around and either go in a circle or sometimes turn back in the opposite direction, all the time thinking they are keeping a straight course. It is as hard to tell why they do this, as why life insurance officials can do such crooked things, and still think that they are honest.

Sebattis Dana, of the Penobscot Indians, once told me that when he was moose hunting with two other Indians, it came on to snow hard and they started for their camp. All thought that they knew the way and they had traveled some time when they came upon the fresh tracks of three men who were traveling in the same direction as themselves. After following for some time, they came to a place where someone had pulled a piece off a rotten stub in passing. Sebattis recognized it as a place where he had slipped and had broken off the stub in recovering himself. A closer inspection showed that they were following their own tracks. They then started again but soon came round to their tracks the second time. Sebattis felt sure that he could go straight, and took the lead, but shortly they were back again to their own tracks. Finally, one of them climbed a tree and could see the lake, near which they camped, close by them; but even then, he had to throw a branch toward it to get a right start. Soon after they reached camp it stopped snowing, and they went back to examine their tracks. Sebattis told me that at the time when he was in the lead he had gone straight toward the lake till within plain sight of it and then all three had turned squarely about and gone back in the direction whence they had come.

I have known of a man coming out close to the edge of a good road and then turning and going back. He did not see the road at all but happened to look up and caught sight of a telegraph wire over his head.

An uncle of mine told me that he had lived at a farmhouse in northern New York all summer. Occasionally he had gone through a piece of woods to visit at another farmhouse. One bright day in the fall he started to go there. The way seemed longer than usual, but he had no doubt but that he was going in the right direction until he came out of the woods and found that he had come out at a place which was strange to him. Seeing a house nearby, he went up to it to inquire the way. It was not until he was in the act of knocking on the door that he realized that he had returned to the same house where he had lived all summer. He had got turned around and this caused familiar things to look strange to him. When a man is in such a state of mind that he cannot tell a main road or a clearing when he sees it, it is useless to talk of his being able to follow any of the many ways which some of these Sherlock Holmeses have written of.

Some of these would-be instructors tell us that there are more branches on the south side of trees, while others tell us that there is more moss on the north side of trees and rocks. Trees branch most toward the open spaces, where there is room to spread their branches, whether it is north or south. Firs and spruces branch very nearly symmetrically, no matter what the situation. As to moss, sometimes trees moss more on one side and sometimes on the other. I have carefully tested the matter with a compass in various locations and find that there is no possible way to get any help as to direction by looking at either limbs or moss, though it is a favorite idea of writers to tell of people finding their way by looking at branches and moss; I have never known of any woodsman being guided in that way. Another tells us that the tips of hemlock and cedar point north, while very recently one claims that the tips of hemlock point toward the east. Now the actual fact is, that no one in the woods can see the tops of trees, even on bright days, unless he is upon a hill above them or in some road or open space. In most cases, when men are lost, it is in dark, rainy, snowy or cloudy days, when there would be no chance to see the treetops; but if they could see them, and it was calm, so that the tops were not bent by the wind, they would find that they bend in all directions. I have walked along in open places and roads testing this by compass, and one might as well rely on which way the leaves fall, as on being guided by the treetops.

Another tells us that the gum is softer on the south side. Now, one may travel miles without seeing any gum at all, and to find it upon both sides of a tree, except upon a spotted line, would be a very unusual thing. In our woods I hardly think that a man could average finding one such tree in a day, and even if he did by chance find one, in cold weather the gum on both sides would be hard. In point of fact, the gum which has recently exuded is soft no matter which side of the tree it is, while the old gum is always hard. Then again, the gum on trees is not confined to the north and south sides of the trees, but is as likely to be found upon the east and west sides if the trees have been wounded on those sides.

Another tells us that by cutting down a tree the rings will be found wider upon the south side. The majority of those out hunting do not carry axes, but if one did, he would find very few cases where the grain of the wood would show any difference. In some cases where a tree stands so its side is fully exposed to the sun there may be a slight difference; but a man might starve to death cutting down trees before he could tell the north from the south. I have traveled the Maine woods in company with as good men as ever traveled these woods, and I never knew any man to be in any way helped by any of these things which so many write of; and those who write so, only show their own ignorance of the woods. Some men I have traveled with never used a compass; some always carried one, but very seldom set it, except in stormy weather; while occasionally a woodsman relies entirely on a plan and compass. Some men seem to be born with a compass in their heads, while some can never learn to travel even with a compass in their hands. A good woodsman finds his way just as an animal does, by a certain kind of instinct. He cannot tell you how he does it or teach you how, but he can do it himself, and knowing that he will hunt all day without troubling his head as to where the camp is. Of course, he is guided some by sun and wind and lay of the land; but it is perfectly surprising what some men can do in finding their way in stormy or cloudy days.

I once separated from an Indian on the top of Bald Mountain near Nictor Lake[105] on the Little Tobique in New Brunswick. He belonged north of the St. Lawrence and was an entire stranger in that part of the country. He was going to look for moose, while I was to take the canoe back after I was done hunting, he coming to the camp at the outlet on foot. The day was fine, but at night grew cloudy and threatened rain. As he failed to come in, I grew anxious and at intervals during the evening fired my rifle with heavy charges to try to guide him in. In the morning it was raining hard. At 9 o'clock in the forenoon I heard someone calling, and, on going across the stream, found Peol.[106] After he had eaten, he told me that he had followed the track of a moose till 5 P.M., then he had started for camp. He traveled till 9. Then he had spotted three trees in line so as to keep the direction, if the wind should change. He built a fire and stood by it all night until at 5 A.M., when it got light enough for him to see to travel; then he

---

[105] Now typically spelled Nictau Lake.
[106] Peol, of this story is Pial [Paul] Antwine Tomah, based on Hardy's 1858 journal, "Notes of a Trip to Tobique." The writing for this 1905 essay, may have been done by memory, and thus the misspelling of the name (or the magazine made a typo). The entry in the journal of where Pial did not return to camp is from Thursday, October 7. Pial is first mentioned when Hardy met him on September 7 at Chamberlain Farm to start out on the hunt.

walked until 9 and had struck the stream only a mile below our camp and followed it up. He estimated that he was sixteen miles from camp when he started back, as he had traveled eight hours to get in. He had no compass, in fact, never carried one, although he always carried a watch. He had eaten nothing except a piece of hard bread since the morning before, and had been out all night with no clothing but pants and a red flannel shirt; yet he did not speak of having had a hard time. He remarked that two owls slept at the same house where he did, and that he traveled by the wind. I have hunted with a number of men who, I think, could have done as well.

I once heard Paul B. Du Chaillu, the noted traveler, say: "On the west coast of Africa, if you fall into the water the sharks shall get you sure; consequently, you had better never fall in!" And so, I would say to those going into the woods, "You had better never get lost."

— Manly Hardy

This essay elicited several responses from readers. Some in support of Hardy's ideas, and some against what they felt were generalizations. However, there are people getting lost in the Maine woods, and no matter how experienced they are, or how close to a trail they may have been, they get disoriented and things go downhill very fast. Stay safe out there.

XXX — Whiskey Jack

⁂

THERE was a recent winter, when on New Year's Day the waves were still lapping at the ice-covered rocks along the shore of Moosehead Lake. The freeze-up was delayed, and the ice-fishing didn't begin until late in January. Once the activity on the ice picked up, Whiskey Jack was there, visiting the fishermen, looking for a handout. From out on the ice, where the shacks and brightly colored tents were stationed, videos began appearing on the internet of the tame fellow eating from the hands of men, women, and children. I say, "fellow," but I doubt the male sex of the species is alone in their poaching, although the nicknames given to the beggar would seem to dictate that is the case. This bird must have the longest list of aliases of any winged visitor to the north woods. The Canada jay (*Perisoreus canadensis*) has been known to be identified by Whiskey Jack, Whiskey John, (or as Whisky), Gray (or grey) jay, moosebird, meat-bird, beef-bird, camp-robber, and gorbie. In Hubbard's *Woods and Lakes of Maine*, the author includes a footnote with the names of Ouiske Jean and Whiskey Johnny.[107]

The nickname, whiskey-jack, may have been taken from Wiskedjak, Wisagatcak, Wisekejack, or other variations of a

---

[107] Hubbard attributes this Indian naming and transition of Montagnais Ouishcatcha^n (in Cree, Ouiskeshauneesh) to Dr. J. Hammond Trumbull, in the *Collections of the Connecticut Historical Society*, Vol. II. p. 44.

word used in the Cree and Algonquian languages to designate a mischievous spirit who liked to play tricks on people.

In this essay by Eckstorm, she specifies a typical limited range for the bird within Maine, with only rare exceptions in the late 1800s and early 1900s being reported south of the typical observed line. Five decades after Eckstorm's essay, E. B. White,[108] in his 1955 essay, "Home-Coming," mentions how a whiskey-jack sighting stirred the Brooklin, Maine community with an article in the paper titled, "UNUSUAL BIRD SEEN." He adds to this unusual sighting that he had seen two of the birds the month prior. Seven years later, in his 1962 postscript addition to this same essay, White includes that "the whiskey-jack showed up again a couple of years ago." He writes how the bird followed him around the cedar swamp, concluding, "the Canada jay looks as though he had slept in his clothes." These mentions are important, because a southern or coastal sighting in Maine was, and still is, unusual for Whiskey-jack.

In addition to the woodlore that Eckstorm covers about the bird, Robert Pike, in *Tall Trees, Tough Men* (1967), relays, "it is one of the pet superstitions of the woodsmen that moose-birds, are the reincarnated souls of dead lumberjacks." He goes on, "You must never harm one of them, even if he snitches a flitch of bacon, or dire evil will befall you."

May you have the luck of experiencing an encounter in the north woods with Whiskey Jack. Whatever he desires, let him

---

[108] E. B. White, most famously the author of *Charlotte's Web*, moved from New York City to Brooklin, Maine and for decades wrote varied, and often humorous, observations from his coastal farm plot near Allens Cove.

have it, for you will be rewarded with amusement during his visit and you can avoid testing the lumberman's superstition.

≱≱≱

Bird = Lore

A BI-MONTHLY MAGAZINE
DEVOTED TO THE STUDY AND PROTECTION OF BIRDS

OFFICIAL ORGAN OF THE AUDUBON SOCIETIES

Vol. IV   JULY — AUGUST, 1902   No. 4

Concerning the Bad Repute of Whiskey John
by
FANNIE HARDY ECKSTORM
Author of *The Bird Book*, *The Woodpeckers*, Etc.

IN these days every bird has his apologist, but I should rather not be the advocate to defend Whiskey John. He is the worst thief, the greatest scoundrel, the most consummate hypocrite abroad in feathers, with his Quaker clothes, his hoary head, his look of patriarchal saintliness. He is a thief, a thief, a thief!

A friendly bird-lover who would loyally whitewash the character of the arch-fiend provided he were a *feathered* biped, argues that to admit of birds having a glimmering of moral sense would make them accountable for their actions in cherry-time, and that therefore the negative must be sustained. The vicious circle in the proof appears at once when we bring forward Whiskey Jack as a bird indubitably lacking moral sense, and inquire what would happen if all other birds were equally defective in their ethical notions. The sum of all the charges against Whiskey Jack is that he knows nothing and cares nothing about morals. Whether he does or does not know the difference between *meum* and *tuum,* he has a decided preference for what is not his own. He steals from pure love of pilfering, and shows not the slightest compunctions of conscience. He steals not alone to satisfy his own wants, but those of his brothers and sisters and wife's relations, and his third, fourth and fifth cousins, and after that he keeps right on stealing for posterity. He takes not only articles for which he has a use and an appetite, but others which he never saw before, doesn't know the uses of, doesn't like the taste of, and can never learn to enjoy or use. I am willing to share generously my cherries and strawberries with the birds; I am ready to divide my last meal of bread and meat with them, but I draw the line at allowing any bird to eat my *soap.* Soap is soap in the Maine woods, forty miles from a store, and even if it were something else it is debatable whether half a cake (of soap) is better for birds than no bread. But, as old Jed Prouty said of the dog that wanted the moon,[109] Whiskey Jack is "cov'tous."

———————————

[109] Fannie Eckstorm always had a way of adding references to stories she had read in her writing, and this is yet another example. The book, "Old Jed Prouty: A Narrative of the Penobscot," (1901) by Richard Golden and Mary Cornelia Francis was based on a play and from additional material gathered in and about the town of Bucksport, Maine. In that town, there was a home, built around 1780, which around 1820 was converted into what became an historic tavern, the *Jed Prouty Tavern and Inn.* In 1986 it was placed on the National Register

If he were a better-known bird his ill-repute would be in everybody's mouth; his isolation saves him. But all fur-hunters and all who travel the great spruce woods, from Atlantic to Pacific, know and revile Whiskey John. He goes by many names, of which this, being only a corruption of the Indian Wis-ka-tjon (but wouldn't one like to know what that means in Indian!) is as complimentary as any. In Maine he is most commonly called the Moose-bird or Meat-bird; in the Adirondacks he is the Camp-robber; in books he is the Canada Jay. If you would know how he looks do not go to the scientific books that tell you every feather on him, but take down your Lorna Doone and turn to those pages where that wily old scoundrel, Counsellor Doone, running away with Lorna's diamond necklace, almost persuades John Ridd that he is a good man cruelly misnamed. Whiskey Jack is the bird counterpart of Counsellor Doone. He looks like him, acts like him and has the same undesirable expertness in acquiring property not his own. Newcomers to the woods dread bears, wolves and snakes. What they fear will never harm them; it is the weak things of the wilderness that are exceeding strong.

---

of Historic Places, and as of the year 2021, it was an assisted living facility. In the book, Old Uncle Jed lets it be known that he has a magic lantern, to which the young ones reply, "Oh, Uncle Jed! Uncle Jed, give it to me!" Jed responds, "Now stop so much hollerin'. I'm ashamed o'ye, bein' so greedy an' graspin', wantin' everythin' thet don't belong ter ye. Don't you know thet's covetousness? Why, ef ye go on l'ke this ye'll all be l'ke th' old yaller dog thet barked fer th' moon." Old Jed goes on to tell the young ones about the dog who barked at everything he wanted, including one rainy night at the moon, when he caught pneumonia and died. According to Old Jed, this was on account of the dog's covetousness.

There is a certain large-winged, tiny-bodied little fly, so feeble and appealing that in pity for his frailty you tenderly brush him aside — and then learn that he is the bloody butcher who is flaying your neck and ears; there is this clear-eyed, mild-mannered, trustful bird, for whose good behavior you would go bonds — until he eats your soap. These two and the mosquito are the real enemies of man in the wilderness.

Suppose that you are paddling along one of the still, thicket-bordered, moose-haunted streams of northern Maine, the "Sis," on Caucomgomoc,[110] for example. There is a whistling and confabulating ashore and down scales a medium-sized gray bird, whitish beneath and with a white forehead which gives him a curiously venerable and bald-headed look. He stretches out his black legs and alights with an uncertain hover on your canoe-bow. "Ca-ca-ca? Who are you anyway?" he inquires, looking boldly at you. You are new to this sort of thing and the woods are big and lonely; it seems like getting into a city to go where nobody cares about you, and this confidence man takes you in at once. He flits ashore and tells the others that is So-and-so, of New York. Then back he comes; he never stays still long anywhere. "Ca-ca-ca? Got any meat today?" says he, seating himself again upon the bow. Perhaps the guide has given you a hint, and this time you bat at him with the paddle and bid him begone for a thief. That hurts his feelings; he puffs out his waistcoat feathers in ruffled

---

[110] In *Hubbard's Guide to Moosehead Lake and Northern Maine*, the name of the stream between Caucomgomoc Lake (T7 R14 WELS) and Round Pond is labeled as, "Sis." My edition of the Maine Gazetteer labels it as "Ciss," which is not the term for indicating a diminutive.

innocence till you forget that it would take half a dozen such thistle-down birds as he to weigh a pound, and he says: "Look at me, do you imagine that a fellow as old and gray-headed and respectable as I am would steal?" You do look at him — a little, stout, white-headed old gentleman with a clear hazel eye, like a superannuated clergyman who had gone into business too late in life to learn the ways of a wicked world, and you apologize profoundly — that is, if you are a novice in the woods; if you have already paid for your introduction to Mr. Whiskey John, you remark, "Pecksniff, get out!" and resort to the argument of the paddle.

He flits away forgiving you; Whiskey Jack is never above such mean revenges. When he comes back, as he is pretty sure to do, it is with the nonchalant impudence of a private detective, "If you don't mind," says he, "I think I'll just take a look at this outfit; I'm a sort of game-warden and have a right to overhaul your baggage." The next minute you hear the guide's paddle bang the middle bar of the canoe. "That there blimey Meat-bird a-stealin' our saddle of deer," he explains briefly.

This time Whiskey John is irritated and he flies off talking jay-talk, a most profane language, threatening to follow you to your camping ground and bring with him every last relative that he has.

He does it, too. When you put your stuff ashore and begin to pitch your tent you know that you have a part of a saddle of deer, a big trout cleaned and split, a Partridge in the leg of one wading boot and a Wood-duck in the other, thrust there hunter-fashion to safe-guard them from accidental loss. You turn your back for a few moments, hear nothing unusual, suspect no mischief; but when you turn again you find the trout is a drabbled rag, rolled in dirt, the roast of venison which was to be the best part of your feast, is riddled above the kidneys (which are the favorite morsel of most meat-eating birds), and both the Duck and the Partridge have been dragged from their concealment and chiseled down the breast till there is nothing left. This is lesson number one. It teaches that the Meat-bird will destroy an incredible amount of meat in a very brief time.

You are now prepared to proceed to lesson number two, which is that if his appetite is limitless yet nothing comes amiss to it. The tent is up: the guide is off to get water from the spring; the fire crackles and the potatoes, boiling in their kettle, are knocking at the cover of it; the bread is baking in the open baker and the nice little collops of venison are lying in a tin plate before the fire all ready for the pan; you lie back on your blanket and dream dreams. Nothing happens till the guide returns, and then you hear a muttered growl about leaving a "sport" to keep a camp. There is the guide, looking at an empty plate, and there on a bush sits a Meat-bird with a very bloody breast. The connection is unmistakable.

Never mind; there is more meat where that came from, and a bird that, in addition to all his other work, has just stolen the dinner for two men cannot be hungry. But he doesn't appear to have lost his interest in your affairs. Instead, he tip-toes around on a limb, with wings and tail half spread, whistling and talking, and no sooner is a fresh supply of meat in the pan than he sweeps down in the smoke and heat and balances a moment on the long handle of the frying-pan, calculating the risks of stealing from the pan. Reluctantly he gives up the project and disappears around the corner of the tent. Presently other things begin to disappear. There is a little hollow in the ground, so that the sides of the tent are not pegged down closely. Entering here, he goes to work within three feet of your elbow, being hidden by a box, and, with the tireless industry which is his only virtue, he applies himself to whatever is nearest. You have some cherished candles, your only light for reading; he drags them off by the wicks. There was a dipper of grease for making pitch; that vanishes. You had pinned a rare bug to a chip; he eats it. You had saved some Duck's wings for the children at home; they are overhauled. The guide left his piece of pork unrolled, and it probably goes off in company with your tobacco, which never turns up after this visitation of Whiskey Jack. When you start to wash up for dinner, there is the rascal eating your soap for dessert! Those who have summered and wintered him say that the only article he has never been seen to steal is kerosene.

"Him eat moccasins, fur cap, matches, anythink," says an Indian to one observer.

As for the amount that they will devour and carry off, there is no likelihood of anyone ever having a patience to equal their — their "cov'tousness," as Jed puts it. There is in this typical account of their actions nothing exaggerated except the probability of its happening in one day.

The Canada Jay is not found everywhere even in Maine. One might camp for years in our woods and never see a Jay, for they are the most local bird that we have in the woods. Roughly speaking, the line of his frontier very nearly coincides with the route of the Canadian Pacific railway where it crosses this state. For example, he is found on the Grand Lakes of St.

Croix,[111] but not on Dobsy and Nicatowis, four ranges of townships to the south. In that region, which seems perfectly adapted to him, I have camped eight weeks; and my father, in the course of twenty-five years, has spent as many months; yet, with one exception, we have neither seen nor heard a Canada Jay in all that wilderness. On collating the experiences of four good observers, I find that they can mention but two instances of a Canadian Jay being seen within fifteen miles of Bangor, and one of these was fully thirty years ago and the other not less than sixty years since; yet hardly more than fifty miles away they are a common resident. Why do they never straggle a short day's journey? Why is it that an omnivorous bird, intelligent, restless, enterprising, fearless, apparently capable of adaptations and certainly attracted by the neighborhood of man, belonging to an order of birds which is eminently civilizable, is so closely restricted in its distribution? There is no climatic barrier; there is no noteworthy difference in the vegetal faunas of places within and without his limits; there is no dietary restriction as in the case of some local birds. Here is a very interesting ornithological puzzle.

The nest and eggs of the Canada Jay I have never seen. A standing offer of two dollars apiece for the eggs, though repeated several years, failed to bring in a single specimen. Woodsmen seem very ignorant of their breeding habits, and the only positive statement that I remember was the remarkable information volunteered by a lumberman that the "Beef-bird" nested and had young every month in the year. It is well known, however, that they nest in March when the

---

[111] Near the Maine-Canada border at Danforth.

snow is still very deep in the woods. The first of June I have seen the young, fully feathered and larger than parents, and with the edges of their bills still yellow. They were a very dark blackish slate, wholly unlike the adult. This plumage seems not to have been generally noticed, though it is worn some time.

On considering the evident reluctance of woodsmen to hunt up the nests of this bird, I have suspected that there may be some superstition connected with the bird similar to that which Mr. L. M. Turner records of the Labrador sub-species. The Indians there believe that "if a person sees the eggs in the nest, and especially if he counts them, some great misfortune will befall him." This is curiously substantiated in Mr. E. W. Nelson's account of the Alaskan sub-species, where he notes that the natives refused large bribes rather than take the risk of angering the bird by stealing its nest. The superstition applies only to the eggs, and is, I suspect, coincident with the distribution of the bird, though I never thought to inquire of our hunters and Indians on the subject. Indeed, unless it were chanced upon, its authenticity as a superstition would be doubtful, as the legend-hunter in Maine has only to state what he wants and he gets all he pays for. The seekers of the marvelous are sure to be satisfied.

How the native hunters always hated Whiskey Jack! They never had a good word for him, and a bullet was their usual greeting. The camper came home to find his hut invaded; the deer-stalker had his carcasses of venison riddled by their sharp bills and unfit for market; the trapper's sable were half-ruined in the traps, and, more provoking yet, his traps were robbed of their bait within five minutes after they had been set. It was hard work to plod all day through the lonesome, snowy wilderness, carrying a heavy bag of bait, and to feel that he was doing nothing but feed these gray wolves in feathers, who robbed him of his chance to get a fisher, lynx or sable almost before he was out of sight. And there is a side to this enmity between the hunter and the Meat-bird that is gruesome. It is years since, but some of us still recollect the tale, of an old outlaw and murderer — more than once a murderer if reports were true — who after haunting the woods for years, a terror to those who crossed his path, fell finally in his turn, the victim of a man as evil as himself. He was shot by his partner and left alone to starve to death in his camp. And after three weeks of utter abandonment and despair, as he saw his end approaching, with no possibility of escaping it, he crept to the cold fireplace and got a black coal with which he scrawled a message on a shred of birch bark. And they found him later, dead and alone, with a tin basin protecting his face, so that, as the writing said, "the Meat-birds might not pick his face after he was dead."[112]

A dread like that, shadowing the last hours of such a man, directing his last words and last act: what a revelation it is of the character of the bird and of the inveterate enmity with which the hunter regards him!

— Fannie Hardy Eckstorm

---

[112] The story related here is of a hermit known as Dirty Donald. In Hubbard's book (noted earlier), Donald's camp was near the Musquacook Lakes and Donald had covered his face to protect it from the snow falling down the chimney. The attack by a meat-bird seems a more plausible explanation. Eckstorm also references Donald in, *Exploring the Maine Woods – The Hardy Family Expedition to the Machias Lakes*.

Facts about Jack:

- The birds live in the northern forest year-round.
- Their chicks are reared in the dead of winter.
- They do not generally breed below 2,000 feet above sea level.
- The diet of a Canada Jay includes berries, eggs, seeds, nuts, fruit, insects, and even small animals.
- They are hoarders and cavities of trees are stuffed with food to sustain them through winter.
- The jay has a sticky saliva that allows them to glue small food items above the snow line for later consumption.
- Jack has been known to enter cabins to steal food.
- They can carry food with their feet, in addition to their bills, a trick unique for a songbird.

On another note:

I found that E. B. White once mentioned Manly Hardy in his writing. In a 1966 essay in *The New Yorker* titled, *Mr. Forbush's Friends*, White goes into great detail on the contents of ornithologist Edward Howe Forbush's three-volume work *Birds of Massachusetts and Other New England States (1929)*. Within the books Forbush added numerous notes of bird sightings submitted by readers, some of which take on an amusing oddity. The contributions number in the many hundreds and White summarizes but a few dozen in his essay. The summarized contribution from Manly Hardy reads:

Mr. Manly Hardy. Camped on island off Maine coast. The discarded red shells of cooked lobsters were all about. Ruby-throated hummingbirds suddenly appeared out of the fog, went from shell to shell under impression they were flowers. 1895.

XXXI — A Secret

by
Anna Boynton Averill

A bird woke in the starlight
And warbled, clear and soft,
A tender little trill.
The dewy linden stirred
And whispered one low word,
And then the night was still.
I leaned out in the stillness —
Out in the dim, sweet night,
And caught the word that fell;
I and the drowsy bird
Were all that ever heard,
And we shall never tell.

Loon at Twilight
(Editor's Collection)

XXXII — The End

I hope you have enjoyed this collection of timeless stories from the Maine north woods. While, the essays only covered a small fraction of the scenery and wildlife, maybe you were transported to the deep woods during your reading.

The expansiveness of the northern regions of the state is so large, exploring it all could take a lifetime. Across the four seasons of the year, those who enjoy the outdoors will find adventure waiting for them. When you are here and the wind howls in the pines, give a thought to if maybe Pamola is sending a storm from Katahdin's peaks. And, if you should pull your canoe onto a gravel bar to have your lunch, keep your eyes out for Whiskey Jack, who will appreciate if you save him a few morsels. In the evening, after you've pitched your tent, search out some poplar that's 'died on the stump,' and give it a try. Above all, take the time to observe the little things that make the out-of-doors what they are – the songs of the birds, the colors in the sky, the sound of a brook, for Fannie would have wanted it that way.

A Personal Note

Fannie Hardy Eckstorm and Anne Boynton Averill

In, *Exploring the Maine Woods – The Hardy Family Expedition to the Machias Lakes*, within the biographical sketch of poet Anna Boynton Averill, I wrote I was unaware of any connection between Fannie Hardy Eckstorm and Averill. I stand corrected, if you will allow the following to count.

Recently I was fortunate enough to purchase an original 1908 printing of Averill's book, Birch Stream and Other Poems. On the title page, there is an inscription, that reads, "Harriet Abbott – 1908 – Presented to Florence H. P. Chase."

Thanks to the assistance from the Fryeburg Historical Society, I discovered, that Abbott and Chase were neighbors. Abbott was a leading citizen of Fryeburg where she was the town clerk for more than twenty years. Early in life she was a teacher in Massachusetts and Maine. Amongst other initiatives, she was a member of the school committee, a charter member of the Fryeburg Woman's Literary Club, and treasurer of the Oxford County Literary Union.

In 1908, the year Abbott gifted the book to a 14-year-old Chase, Abbott was 46 years of age. Abbott's obituary noted, "She has always interested herself in the affairs of young people and will be gratefully remembered for her interest." It is no wonder then that Abbott had given a young Chase the book of Averill's poems. Chase, for her part, became an artist whose paintings were well-known in the Fryeburg area.

So, what is the connection to Eckstorm? Abbott lived in Fryeburg, a long journey from Brewer in those days – even considering the railroad connections at the time. However, it turns out, Eckstorm and Abbott, aside from being close in age, had many common interests and knew one another. The September 11, 1913 Journal of Education reported a meeting was held in Rockland of, "a society to promote the study of various sciences in Maine." Of the five committee officers, Miss Harriet Abbott of Fryeburg was treasurer and secretary, and Fannie Hardy Eckstorm of Brewer was listed as author and lecturer on ornithology. The two women shared more than a passion for educating the young, as we also already know that

Eckstorm was a founding member of the Brewer Public Library, and served as superintendent of the Brewer schools for a year. They also shared a love of birds. In Abbott's obituary, a line reads, "She was an authority on birds and had a large acquaintance among bird lovers all over New England." Abbott was a frequent contributor to the monthly, Nature and Culture. An essay she published in 1910 was titled, *Bird Study in Public Schools*, in which she describes the taking of the student body through an education and observation course on birds, with students excited to get to 'class' by 5 A.M. I suspect Eckstorm and Abbott would have had a good deal to talk about, particularly pertaining to the out-of-doors; a subject which Averill so often depicted in her poems.

Thus, my completely by chance selection of Averill's poems into the books of Eckstorm's essays, turns out to have a very interesting connection. I feel extremely fortunate to have stumbled across an original of Averill's book, doubly so for the inscription within. Maine certainly is a small town.

1908 Printing
Gift from Harriet Abbott
to
Florence H. P. Chase

About Tommy Carbone

Tommy Carbone lives in Maine with his wife and two daughters. He studied electrical engineering and earned a Ph.D. in engineering management.

He writes from a one room cabin, on the shores of a lake, that is frozen for almost six months out of the year, and moose outnumber people three to one.

His first novel, "*The Lobster Lake Bandits – Mystery at Moosehead*," has made those 'from away' want to visit Maine. It's a big state – come explore.

BOOKS FROM MAINE'S NORTH WOODS

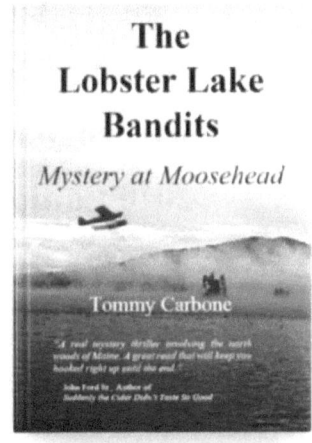

A Maine Novel

The second novel in the

Moosehead

Mystery

series

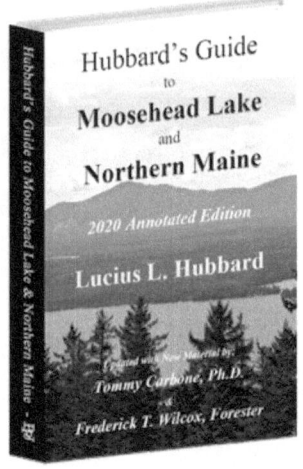

Hubbard's Guide
to exploring
Northern Maine.
2020 Edition

Hubbard's
adventure through
Maine to Canada.
2020 Edition

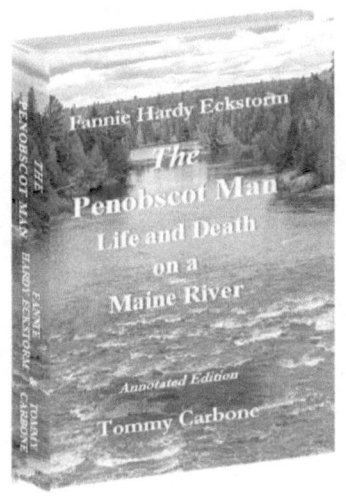

**The Penobscot Man
Life and Death on a
Maine River**
A new title Annotated
Edition with content
not included in the
original book.

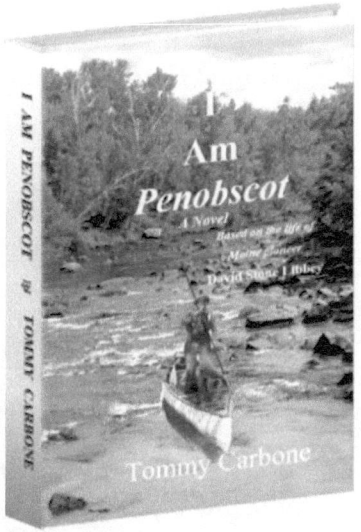

**I am
Penobscot**
A novel based on the
life of Maine pioneer
David Stone Libbey –
river-driver, miner,
Civil War soldier, and
writer under the pen
name of Penobscot.

"Thomas S. Steele's Maine Adventures."
An edition of Steele's two books about the Maine North Woods and excerpts from
John M. Way's 1874 book,
"A Guide to Moosehead Lake and Northern Maine."

Based on the writing of

Fannie Hardy Eckstorm

this memoir is a wonderful tale of the Maine woods and history from the 1800s.
Read more Eckstorm stories in: